T3-BSJ-602

Building Up Your Congregation

Help from Tested Business Methods

BUILDING UP YOUR CONGREGATION

Help from Tested Business Methods

BY

Willard A. Pleuthner

OF BATTEN, BARTON, DURSTINE AND OSBORN
ADVERTISING AGENCY

WILCOX & FOLLETT CO.

New York CHICAGO *Toronto*

All of the author's royalties from this book will be given to interfaith religious charities.

Second Printing, 1950

Manufactured in the U. S. A.
by H. Wolff Book Mfg. Co., Inc.

DEDICATION

To the memory of my father,
Augustus J. Pleuthner,
a faithful church member. Some
of the suggestions in this book
are developed from his reflections.

ACKNOWLEDGMENTS

The Author sincerely appreciates the help and inspiration of the following people in writing this book:

W. A. Benfield, Jr.—Vice-President of the Louisville Presbyterian Seminary

Samuel McCrea Cavert—Secretary of the Federal Council of Churches

Rt. Rev. Edward R. Welles, Bishop of Episcopal Diocese of West Missouri

Ralph Stoody—Executive Director of Commission on Public Information of the Methodist Church

Stanley Stuber of Church World Service

Lewis Shank of Goodwill Industries in Washington, D.C.

Alex F. Osborn, Bruce Barton, Carl Spier, John Johns, Dale Casto, Robert N. King, John Caples, Harry Olsen, and Evelyn Strittmatter of Batten, Barton, Durstine and Osborn, Inc.

Others who co-operated include: Donald M. Wright . . . Richard T. Baker . . . Eleanor Inman . . . and the many church-workers who supplied ideas and plans to make this book more useful.

Without the assistance, advice, and suggestions of all these people this book would have been incomplete. Daniel A. Poling, Editor of "Christian Herald," co-operated in granting permission to reprint two articles which were written for that outstanding religious magazine. These are: "Let's Face It" . . . and "Dangerous Dignity of Church Boards."

The author is deeply indebted to the leading ministers and layworkers who gave their valuable time to read over his manuscript. Their volunteered statements were a real encouragement during that long process of getting a book published.

CONTENTS

PART I

Increasing Attendance at Services

PART II

Increasing Financial Support

PART III

Publicizing Your Church

PART IV

A Word to the Wise

PART

I

Increasing Attendance at Services

Prayer for the Reader

Dear Heavenly Father bless and strengthen Thy servant, the reader of this book. Grant him an open-minded understanding of its ways of bringing more and more souls into closer contact with Thy love for all mankind. May he find through this book ways of removing the barriers which keep many of Thy children from knowing the peace which passeth understanding.

1

Wanted—More Exposures to Christian Ministry

PEOPLE today, more than ever before, need the teachings of Jesus Christ. They are faced with problems—gigantic, complex, and world-wide—which can only be solved through a Christian approach and an adherence to Christian principles. Whether the world travels the path-way to peace or takes the road to World War III will be determined by the number of people who follow the teachings of the Prince of Peace.

Today's problem of converting more people to the Christian way of life is history's greatest challenge to the Church. Only a phenomenal growth in the Church's influence and membership can save civilization from destroying itself. Only through Christians all over the world can we be sure that the new atomic power will be used to serve instead of destroy mankind. Therefore, we should all work unceasingly to live better Christian lives and to bring more people into the Church.

The basic objective of the clergy is the spiritual quality of the congregation. The primary questions in their minds are: "Is my min-istry, my message, getting through?" "Is it building and lifting the souls of persons the way it should?" Churches should be interested *first* in the quality of their members' lives and only second in the quantity of their members. They should not be interested in mere growth in membership. Churches should not cater to the so-called "popular appeal" at the expense of deep spiritual growth. The seminaries and the denominational organizations are doing an outstanding job in helping the clergy to enhance the spiritual life and spiritual influence of their congregations.

To take the fullest advantage of the efforts of our pastoral leaders, as many people as possible should be exposed to their ministry and message. Isn't it difficult to influence a person unless that individual comes in close contact with the Church and Christ's teaching? Reading a newspaper report of a sermon is a poor substitute for hearing it at firsthand and sharing in the service. Even listening to the broadcast of a church service is not to be compared with attending the service personally. There is no exposure to Christ's teachings as effective and as complete as attendance at an inspiring church service. Therefore, it seems logical that to convert those outside the Church, we should make specific plans to get nonmembers to attend Sunday services. To influence a person you have to focus his attention on your message. In religion this takes place best in church. Thus in one way, the growth of a church depends on getting more and more individuals to attend more and more services. The more of these exposures to Christ's teachings, the more people will join and support His churches.

Naturally, these plans should not run counter to the feelings of the faithful, who are the backbone of church attendance. However, the plans in this idea manual have been carried out without disturbing regular congregations. In fact, most members welcomed those activities which brought into their church friends and neighbors who ordinarily did not attend.

2

Dangerous Dignity of Church Boards

IS your board's dangerous dignity dwarfing your church's progress? That question combines dignity and progress in the same sentence. Seldom do these two words go together in actual life . . . at least in their extremes. Too much dignity usually means too little progress. An examination of the reasons why churches show so little progress often reveals too much respect for dignity.

Plans for aggressive action or progressive steps are often turned down by a church's board as being "undignified." The board members seem to forget that according to the New Testament, thousands of followers were attracted to Christ by what would today be considered undignified miracles—undignified acts of healing. Can you imagine the average church board being asked to approve such miracles as the turning of water into wine, or feeding the multitude on two fishes and five loaves of bread?

Deacons, elders, trustees, or wardens forget that the most dignified thing in the world is a corpse. One of the most undignified is a growing baby. Too many churches are like the former and too few like the latter.

One reason for the dangerous dignity of many church boards is found in its membership. On the boards of urban churches there are often too many bankers, lawyers, doctors, and retired businessmen, and too few sales managers, advertising men, and active business executives on the way up the ladder of success. As a result, there is little aggressive salesmanship-thinking to "season" the conservatism of men who have to be conservative to succeed in their nonselling professions. Yet, today our churches need aggressive selling leadership more than any organization in the world. The yearly gains in membership show that many churches are not keeping abreast of national growth. They are being by-passed by competing activities which grow bigger and bigger through successful methods of selling.

Another factor in the dangerous dignity of some church boards is their self-perpetuating membership. An inner clique stays in power continuously A few leading families monopolize the officerships. Yes, a certain degree of continuity in trusteeship is a good thing. However, to be truly democratic, members should be elected for three- or four-year terms.

The more progressive and open-minded churches realize that their church board is not complete, is not truly representative unless it includes at least one representative of Labor. Like sales and advertising executives, labor leaders are usually conspicuous by their absence. This tends to make the church seem like a "one-class institution." One of the best places for management and labor leaders to get to know and trust each other is on a church board. You may not have a labor leader in your congregation. However, any member who belongs to a union or is a "shop steward" can bring to the board the benefits of Labor's point of view.

Right now you may be saying, "What's wrong with successful bankers, competent lawyers, and professional men? Why are they responsible for the church's dangerous dignity?" The answer is obvious. Most of these board members achieved success by having people come to them for help and not by going out and selling their services to people who needed them. Today, most churches cannot grow unless they stop waiting for people to come to them, and take a more progressive attitude toward getting new members and increasing church attendance.

Churches should go out and sell their exclusive God-given advantages to the general public. The Church has more happiness, more peace and contentment, more true joy and satisfaction to offer than any merchandise or service advertised in full-color pages in national magazines.

Yet the average church shuns most of those successful forms of planning, selling, and advertising which have made business grow bigger year by year. They are classed as "undignified" by the conservative members of the church's board. Well, let's turn our backs on this dangerous dignity and take a look at some of these proven ways to grow, to attract and influence more people.

3

Establishing a Yearly Goal of Growth

MOST of the methods of building larger congregations fall into the following three classifications:

1. Establishing a yearly goal of growth in church attendance and membership.
2. Organizing definite plans for achieving the desired yearly growth.
3. Maintaining accurate, comparative records showing whether or not the goals are being achieved (and how quickly or slowly).

Now let's look at the problem of "Yearly Goal of Growth" through the eyes of a business doctor. How would your church answer these clinical questions?

(a) Have you a yearly goal for increased church attendance?
Yes ( ) No ( )

(b) Have you a yearly goal for increased church membership?
Yes ( ) No ( )

(c) Are these objectives explained to the entire church?
Yes ( ) No ( )

(d) Are any definite plans made to achieve the goal?
Yes ( ) No ( )

(e) Who makes these plans and sells them to the members and organizations?
Professional men ( ) Salesmen ( )

Where denominations have considered these questions, and have worked out plans to increase their membership, the results have been tangible. If your church has not set up its individual goal for yearly growth, this should be done at once.

The Baptists are one of the denominations that establishes definite goals of yearly growth. Their local congregations have been told how these objectives will be obtained. The Roman Catholics also establish a progressive program for increasing their parishes.

The Presbyterian Church (Northern) is another denomination that has set up definite goals for its evangelism. Under the fine title of "New Life Movement," the Presbyterians have established the following objectives for a three-year period:

300 new churches
1,000,000 new members

More than 100,000 laymen are being recruited and trained as evangelists. Through their efforts, the invitation to attend church has changed from a general, "Come worship with us soon?" to a specific, "This coming Sunday we have a special service. Will you join us?"

The successful sales executive is constantly comparing the growth of his company's business with that of competition and the industry as a whole. He is not satisfied unless the percentage of yearly increase for his concern is as large as any competitor, and is larger than the industry as a whole.

Many businesses aim for a 10% increase in normal years. Of course, this gain is not secured by every business in every year. Yet most successful businesses have found that unless an organization works for a definite increase, it doesn't stand still—but slips backward. It is better to aim for a 10% gain and only obtain a 6% increase than to coast along with the status quo.

Shouldn't the clergy and their boards take the same constructive and progressive attitude as these successful businessmen? Shouldn't each church want to attract new members in at least the same proportion as the national average for the denomination? Parishes with unusual advantages and unusual growth opportunities should not be satisfied with just the average national growth. They should want to better the average year after year. How can your church measure its growth? All you do is to find out the number by which, for instance, your 1950 membership was greater than 1949. Next, figure the percentage gain over your 1948 membership. Then compare that percentage with the national gain for your denomination, and other denominations.

Thanks to *Christian Herald* magazine, comparative records of church membership are made available every year. Here are the figures for the membership of Protestant denominations of 50,000 or more for the years 1949 and 1948.

Protestant Religious Bodies With Membership over 50,000	*Members 1949*	*Members 1948*	*Percent of Gain*
Methodist	8,792,569	8,651,062	1.6
Southern Baptist	6,761,265	6,491,981	4.1
National Baptist Convention, U.S.A., Inc.	4,385,206	4,385,206	
National Baptist Convention of America	2,594,521	2,580,921	
Presbyterian (U.S.A.)	2,401,849	2,330,136	3.1
Protestant Episcopal	2,297,989	2,228,270	3.1
United Lutheran Church	1,814,172	1,814,172	
Disciples of Christ	1,738,605	1,714,796	1.4
Northern Baptist Convention	1,583,360	1,583,360	
Lutheran Missouri Synod	1,569,364	1,519,952	3.3
Congregational Christian	1,184,661	1,184,661	
African Methodist Episcopal	1,066,301	816,578	30.6
Latter Day Saints	980,347	947,855	3.4
Churches of Christ	814,200	682,172	19.4
Evangelical Lutheran	757,352	757,352	
Evangelical and Reformed	714,583	714,583	
Evangelical United Brethren	711,537	707,326	.6
American Lutheran	692,567	646,605	7.1
Presbyterian (U.S.)	653,594	638,652	2.3
African M. E. Zion	520,175	527,350	
Augustana Evangelical Lutheran	439,231	422,646	3.9

Colored Methodist Episcopal	381,000	381,000	
Church of God in Christ	340,530	340,530	
American Baptist Association	313,817	245,861	27.6
Evangelical Lutheran Joint Synod of Wisconsin and Other States	297,922	288,355	3.3
Assemblies of God	275,000	273,147	.7
National Association of Free Will Baptists	255,127	255,127	
Seventh Day Adventists	229,945	222,619	3.3
Church of the Nazarene	220,042	213,188	3.2
Salvation Army	215,094	215,094	
United Presbyterian of N.A.	213,810	205,677	4.
Church of the Brethren	185,088	185,799	
Reformed Church in America	179,085	178,356	.4
Christian Reformed	142,818	138,321	3.3
Latter Day Saints (Reorganized)	121,745	128,849	
Societies of Friends	113,013	113,842	
Church of God (Cleveland)	106,490	96,049	10.9
Church of God (Anderson)	105,022	96,736	8.6
Federated Churches	88,411	88,411	
General Association of Regular Baptist Churches	85,000	85,000	
Cumberland Presbyterian	80,236	78,009	2.9
United American Free Will Baptists	75,000	75,000	
American Unitarian Association	74,447	71,419	4.2
Primitive Baptists	69,157	69,157	
Independent Fundamental Churches of America	65,000	65,000	
Universalist Church of America	62,927	44,349	41.9
Pentecostal Church of God of America	60,000	68,000	
International Church of the Four Square Gospel	59,897	66,611	
National Baptist Evangelical Life and Soul Saving Assembly of U.S.A.	56,934	70,843	
Mennonite Church	56,746	54,729	3.7
Lutheran Free Church	54,608	54,608	
Evangelical Mission Covenant of America	51,009	49,590	2.9

Even if the one-year gain of your church equals the average for the denomination, you should not be satisfied. For the average of the denomination includes the small gains of many churches which are not progressing as fast as they should. The average gain in some denominations is too low because the total figures contain parishes which have ceased to exist actively, but must be counted until the property is sold.

There are some churches that have shown abnormal gains because of unusual growth in their city or neighborhood population. Other congregations have a small population on which to build. In either case, churches should use every sound and tested method to build up their congregations to the greatest possible percentage of their local population potentials. By having church services which satisfy and inspire the souls of men, by properly promoting these services and activities to members and the unchurched, they can obtain "S.R.O." congregations. Yes, there is every reason why successful churches, like successful plays, should have "Standing Room Only" attendance. Certainly Jesus had many occasions when his listeners were so many that they stood and forgot any physical fatigue.

4

Why People Get Out of the Habit of Attending Church

SUCCESSFUL businesses learn to avoid losing customers by finding out why customers stop buying. Then they correct the adverse conditions. Churches can use the same technique to stop losing members to other churches, or losing the regular church attendance of members.

What are some of the "reasons" why some people say they stop going to church regularly?

1. Too many requests for special funds—too many tickets to buy.
2. Too many requests to attend or join church social activities.
3. Regular members "kid" or "roast" the irregular member when he or she appears in church. Remarks such as the following annoy the irregulars and keep them away: "You must be sick or afraid you are going to die." "What's the matter? We only see you on Christmas and Easter."
4. The hymns are unfamiliar.
5. The church gives no special reason for attending most services. There is no special personal appeal to specific groups of people to attend on definite Sundays.
6. The minister fails to keep up his calls on families in the church.
7. Overhospitable churches put "greeters" at the end of every aisle and at each door. To get out of the church, each visitor must be welcomed and "greeted." Some people dislike this. So leave one door, one aisle free for them.

After reading this list, you will see why quotation marks were put around "reasons." For some of them seem to be quite superficial, in fact, just plain excuses. However, it is true that many of these nonmembers like the Church—try to follow Christ's way—but just got out of the habit of attending Sunday services.

Looking at the situation from another viewpoint, many people do not attend church regularly because they cannot, by themselves, reconcile religion with present-day secular life. Or they find the ritual meaningless. Both of these real reasons can be changed by an inspired minister, a devout congregation, and church services which give people something specific to live by in their week-day world.

The above reasons do not apply to all churches. There may be special local or parish reasons for nonattendance. The best way to find out the facts on this problem is to make a local study. Have trained survey reporters call on a cross section of nonattenders. The local newspaper can put you in touch with men or women who have experience in making surveys. In these calls, a questionnaire should be used. In addition, valuable information will be uncovered in the miscellaneous comments made by the respondents. Naturally, the interviews should be made among both men and women.

A good basic questionnaire for this study has been developed by Robert N. King, in charge of research for Batten, Barton, Durstine and Osborn, Advertising Agency. Mr. King's questions are as follows:

1. In what church or faith were you brought up?..............
2. Have you attended a local church of that denomination?......
   Yes ( ) No ( )
3. About how many times per year do you attend church?.......
4. How does it happen that you do not attend more frequently?
   ....
5. What could churches do to make you want to attend services more frequently?..
6. Miscellaneous comment..

Local conditions will suggest additional questions. The sex and approximate age of respondent should be recorded on each interview.

The above questionnaire is designed to be used in interviewing people who are known to be infrequent churchgoers. They include the perennials who attend only on Christmas and Easter. When this survey is done on a house-to-house basis, the same questions are logical. In this case, the survey could be done under the local council of churches, or a group of churches in the same neighborhood. The prospective respondents could be found by getting a house-to-house list of telephone subscribers and then crossing off the names of regular churchgoers. This survey should be followed up with a recruiting drive for church attendance and church membership.

There is another reason for nonattendance or infrequent attendance which does not apply to most churches. That is the small amount of missionary work done by or sponsored by the parish. In this case, some people give as a reason (or an alibi) for their nonattendance the fact that the church spends too much of its time, energy, and funds on its own members and is not spreading the gospel to foreign lands or helping the poor within the city. Right or wrong, these churches are considered more of a religious club than an organization carrying out God's work at home and abroad.

5

Know Your Congregation as Business Knows Its Customers

SUCCESSFUL business firms have grown by finding out everything they could about major factors, such as the following:

1. Present customers
2. Past customers
3. Why new customers are won
4. Potential customers
5. Statistics on increase or decrease in customers
6. Frequency of customer purchases
7. What satisfied customers like about the company
8. What dissatisfied customers dislike about the company

This same type of information can help a church grow and become more successful in influencing its members and the community as a whole.

In many churches the vital statistics on church membership have not been properly audited. The parish lists are woefully padded. People have left the church to attend other churches without asking for a formal transfer. Hence their names usually stay on the former church lists and membership rolls. A good time to correct this false situation is in the summer months when the church office generally has less to do. A letter should be sent to all borderline nonattending members from the minister. This letter should express the desire to keep the member's name on the parish roll, but should state that the church wants to make its list 100% accurate. Therefore, would the recipient please sign an attached post card stating that he or she desires to have his or her name retained on the official membership list? Wrong addresses and lack of information on the family can be corrected at the same time. People who do not fill out the stamped self-addressed post cards are then removed from the parish rolls. Through this checkup, some churches have discovered that up to one-third of their membership list was deadwood.

Here is the information which every church should have and should review at regular intervals:

1. Comparison of each Sunday's attendance with the same Sunday of the preceding year.
2. Accumulated attendance at the Sunday services for the year. This accumulated attendance figure overcomes the discrepancy caused by the fact that the date for special church days like Easter varies year by year. Individual Sunday attendance and accumulated attendance figures for the year to date should be given to the minister every Monday.
3. Sunday school attendance compared with same Sunday last year.
4. Year-to-year comparison of number of people who have joined the church.
5. Year-to-year comparison of people who have left the church and joined other parishes. Why did they leave your church?
6. Year-to-year comparison of average pledges. If this average is standing still or going down, something is radically wrong and should be changed.
7. Breakdown of congregation by these age groups:

Number	*Group*	*% of Total*
....	Sunday School Pupils	....
....	16 to 20 years old	....
....	21 to 30 years old	....
....	31 to 40 years old	....
....	41 to 50 years old	....
....	51 to 60 years old	....
....	61 to 70 years old	....
....	71 and over	....

The percentage of the total congregation in these age groups will show a minister and the board whether the church is growing enough in younger members to more than overcome deaths of older members. It will indicate whether the church is converting its teen-age Sunday school members into regular church members. It will show whether the Younger Marrieds are staying in your congregation or going to some other church.

If the statistics for your church indicate a loss of members in any age group, have someone ask a representative number of that age group why they left the church. Then make plans to correct the conditions which caused their leaving. If your congregation is not showing a 5 to 10% gain each year, find out what is wrong. A church must grow to stay alive. A church which is just standing still will sooner or later start shrinking in membership and influence. No progressive church should be satisfied with its attendance unless it has two well-attended services every Sunday. Reuben Youngdahl, the outstanding pastor of the Mount Olivet Lutheran Church in Minneapolis, has built up the congregation so that three identical services are held every Sunday. One strength of the Roman Catholic churches lies in the fact that each parish has enough communicants to support several morning services every Sunday. There is no reason why Protestant denominations should not achieve similar growth.

It is sound planning to have a meeting of your minister and board regularly (not less than every four months) on ways and means to build up your church attendance. At the time, review the comparative statistics and plan special events to bring more people into your church more frequently. That's the same technique which successful businesses use to grow bigger year after year. Detailed suggestions for attendance-building special events are given in chapter 7.

For example, you may find the boys and girls who go away to school do not come home regular "attenders." This is a serious problem. These boys and girls represent the potential leaders and future strength of your church. You can help assure the church attendance of youth by supporting some organization like the "Church Society for College Work." Chapter 8 explains how this society works to maintain church attendance of away-from-home students.

Some churches have attendance statistics compiled by a special committee. The report is presented to the minister and board twice a year. Any activity which is not producing the desired results or does not have a satisfactory following is carefully examined. Where necessary, special committees are appointed to make a study of the situation and to develop recommendations for its correction.

An outstanding example of knowing your congregation is the survey planned and directed by Bishop G. Bromley Oxnam, head of the Methodist Church in New York City. Bishop Oxnam's study included all the people in Brooklyn. The revealing figures showed the membership of all faiths and how much they have increased or decreased. Population trends by races were charted to indicate the changing potential. Sunday-school attendance was analyzed; congregations were broken down into age groups. The pledges and total church support were also shown by age groups. This comprehensive study gave Bishop Oxnam, his ministers, and their boards a complete detailed picture of their problems and opportunities. Other denominations and/or city councils of churches could make similar surveys to the great advantage of all concerned.

The Lutheran Laymen's League conducted a survey of people who listen to their radio program, "The Lutheran Hour." Filled-out questionnaires were received from 9,678 persons. Those listeners who wrote that they did not attend church regularly were asked to give the reason. Here is the summary of the replies.

Distance	492	or	5%
Work	495		5%
Illness	973		10%
Nonmemberships	57		.59%
Other reason	520		5.61%
No reason given	7,141		73.8%
TOTAL	9,678		100%

Note that the biggest percentage, 73.8%, did not give any reason. Among this large group are your fellow-townspeople—your friends and neighbors. Most of them are just waiting to be asked—waiting to be sold on worshiping with you—in your church.

NOTE:

On the following page you will find the first of a series of plan sheets. Similar plan sheets follow other chapters in this book. They are designed to make it easy and convenient for you to start right away to carry out in your church, the ideas and suggestions about which you are reading.

Plan sheets are more fully discussed in the last chapter of the book, and you will find that there is a duplicate of each plan sheet at the back of the book, perforated so that you can tear them out.

Don't delay in taking this important "first step." Get a pencil right now. Be ready to write in your plans for using these tested methods.

PLAN SHEET

Essential Information on Congregations

1. Official Number of Contributing Members

Year	*Number of Members*	*Gain or Loss over Preceding Year*
19	....	....
19	....	....
19	....	....
19	....	....
19	....	....

2. New Members of Congregation

Year	*Adults*	*From Sunday School*	*Total Gain*
19	....	....	....
19	....	....	....
19	....	....	....
19	....	....	....
19	....	....	....

3. Members Lost to Congregation

Year	*Deaths*	*Transfers to Other Churches*	*Members Who Stopped Contributing*	*Total of All Losses*
19	....	....	....	....
19	....	....	....	....
19	....	....	....	....
19	....	....	....	....

4. Size of Sunday School

Year	*Registered Members of the Schools*	*Gain or Loss over Previous Year*
19	....	....
19	....	....
19	....	....
19	....	....

5. Attendance at Church Services

Year	*Average Attendance at Sunday Services*	*Gain or Loss*
19	....	....
19	....	....
19	....	....
19	....	....

6

Survey of Congregation Uncovers Wealth of Sermon Material

THE clergy have one of the most difficult tasks in the world . . . and one of the most rewarding. In addition to being the operating head of a busy institution . . . calling on the sick and troubled . . . marrying, burying and baptizing . . . attending meetings . . . the minister must prepare a sermon for each Sunday service. These sermons have to be different . . . appeal to different types of people . . . offer solutions to different problems . . . and give inspiration to the entire congregation.

One of the real difficulties of the clergy is to decide on the sermon subject, to determine what can be said that will be of greatest help to the parishioners. Dr. Albert G. Butzer, Minister of Westminster Church in Buffalo, New York, solved this basic problem in the logical way used by a successful business. Dr. Butzer wrote a letter to all members of the parish asking them to tell him what they thought and believed in their personal religion, and in regard to the larger problems of our day. Here is the letter and some questions used in this "sermon-material survey."

Dear Member of Westminster:

For almost fifteen years now I have been highly privileged to be the minister of our parish. Very often I have wondered just what our people honestly think and believe in their personal religion and in regard to the larger problems of our day in the light of our Christian faith.

After considering the matter for several years, I finally have decided to give a series of addresses at the midweek services on the Wednesday evenings during Lent, based on the answers received to the enclosed questionnaire. As a personal favor to me, and as a definite contribution from you, I am asking you to answer frankly all the questions. Husbands and wives may make a joint reply, if they so desire. Our young people will be given this questionnaire at one of their meetings. Those away at school and college will have a questionnaire mailed to them.

Please *do not* sign your name, so as to make your answers as factual as possible, and that the series of addresses may be free from anything personal.

If I receive almost a 100% response from our people, I am sure the series of addresses based on the answers to the questionnaire will be of greatest interest and value to all of us. So please—*please* fill out the enclosed questionnaire as soon as possible and return it to me in the enclosed envelope. I shall be deeply grateful for your prompt and sincere co-operation.

Faithfully yours,

Attached to the letter was a self-addressed return envelope and a questionnaire, part of which follows. (Note: Naturally more space was given in which to answer some questions than is shown here.)

I. FAITH IN GOD AND CHRIST

(a) Is your faith in God strong?............weak?............
(b) What is your deepest source of doubt concerning God?......
(c) What helps you most to believe in God?..................
(d) Do you believe God is personal?...... all-powerful?...... all-knowing? ....

(e) What difference does it make whether or not we believe in God? . . . .
. . . .

(f) Is your faith in Christ as the divine Son of God strong? . . . . . weak? . . . .

(g) Is your faith in the divinity of Christ dependent on:
  (1) His virgin birth? . . . .
  (2) His performance of miracles? . . . .

(h) How does Christ save men from sin? . . . .

(i) To test yourself on the life of Christ, answer the following ten questions without consulting the Bible or any other help:
  (1) Which gospel mentions the following at the birth of of Christ? The shepherds . . . . . The wise men . . . . .
  (2) In which town was Jesus brought up? . . . .
  (3) Name six of the twelve disciples . . . .
  (4) In which gospel is the Sermon on the Mount most fully recorded? . . . .
  (5) Write one of the Beatitudes . . . .
  (6) Name three parables of Jesus . . . .
  (7) Name three miracles performed by Jesus . . . .
  (8) Name three women prominent in the life of Jesus . . .
  . . . .
  (9) Which disciple denied Jesus? . . . .
  Which Roman official tried Jesus? . . . .
  (10) Name three of the seven last utterances of Jesus from the cross . . . .

II. PRAYER

(a) Is your faith in prayer strong? . . . . weak? . . . .

(b) Do you have regular periods of daily prayer? . . . .

(c) For what do you pray most frequently? . . . .

(d) Do you believe in praying for the weather? . . . .
Material things? . . . . People far away? . . . .
Physical health? . . . .

(e) Do you have grace regularly before meals? . . . .

(f) Were you brought up in a home with family prayers? . . . .

(h) Do you believe prayer can be effective?....................
(1) In industrial relations?..........................
(2) For world peace?.............................

III. THE CHURCH

(a) What percentage of Sundays in the year do you attend church?
....

(b) If you attend regularly, what makes you do so?............
(c) If you seldom attend church, is it because
(1) Personal circumstances honestly make it difficult to attend?...
(2) You benefit little by attending?.................
(3) The broadcasting of our services sometimes cause you to stay at home?..............................
(d) What suggestions have you for improving our Sunday morning services?..
(e) What are your three most favorite hymns?................
(f) Is there a particular subject on which you would like to have a sermon?...
(g) If you have children in the Church School, would you favor more or less
(1) Bible study?........ (2) Memory work?........
(3) Home preparation?............ (4) Visual aids in teaching? ....

IV. THE KINGDOM OF GOD ON EARTH

(a) Should a Christian pulpit deal with social, economic, and international problems?................................
(b) If Jesus were on earth today would He "side" with labor or management, or try to bring them together?...............
(c) If a fine family of Negroes asked to be received into membership of our church, would you approve?.................
Negroes are moving into the area around Westminster House. Should we keep the House for white people only?.... Or try to mix the two?...... Or eventually make it a Negro Settlement House?..

(d) Do you think it was right for America to use the atom bomb in the war?..
Should we make an unconditional surrender of it immediately to the United Nations?..........................
(e) Do you believe the United Nations will be able to prevent a third world war?.................................

V. IMMORTALITY

(a) Is your faith in life after death strong?...... weak?......
(b) Do you believe in the resurrection of the physical body of Christ?..
(c) Do you believe there is a hell of eternal punishment?.......
(d) Do you believe there is a heaven of eternal bliss?...........
(e) Do you ever pray for loved ones or friends who have died?...
(f) Do you believe the dead can communicate with us?.........
(g) Do you think it makes any difference in *this* life whether we believe in life after death?.............................

After reading over the above questionnaire, any preacher or lay worker can realize why Dr. Butzer's addresses, based on this study, were among the most helpful ever given in Westminster Church. And the attendance broke several records! Why? Because the congregation knew that Dr. Butzer's preaching was based on a full knowledge of *their* thoughts, *their* beliefs, and *their* ideas of current problems. When such a sermon-material study can get more people into church for midweek service, think what it could do to increase attendance at your regular Sunday services!

7

Special Services
How They Help Increase Attendance

THERE are several plans which can help your church increase its attendance at regular services. This new set makes a special appeal to definite groups of members or nonmembers. These new special services are to be in addition to the church's regular services on Christmas, Easter, or during Lent. They increase attendance in between major church Sundays of the year.

Right here some readers may ask: "Why suggest some *new,* special Sunday services when our church already has so many?" This is a logical question, and naturally some congregations will prefer just to follow the regular liturgical calendar of their own denomination.

The special Sunday services about to be described were developed from the techniques used by successful and growing businesses. Like business promotions, they have a *specific* and *understandable* appeal to definite groups of prospects . . . prospective churchgoers. Their appeals are basic, everyday ones which do not require an understanding of church Holy Days or ecclesiastical celebrations. In using these special Sundays to invite nonchurchgoers to attend your church, you don't have to explain at length the meaning of the special Sunday service. Like successful business promotions, no involved explanations are necessary.

Just like business-building campaigns, these special Sunday services will bring new faces into church. These services will definitely expose certain people to the ministry of your church who otherwise would not have attended. Experience shows that a definite percentage of these "special guests" at these special Sundays will attend your church again and again. A definite percentage of these repeat-attenders will become members of your congregation. Exactly what percentage of special guests will come back again, and exactly what percentage join the church depend on many factors, including: the music, how guests are "greeted," the atmosphere of the church, their impressions of the congregation, the depth of feeling created by the service and sermon. No special promotion takes the place of these basic factors.

The primary function of these special Sunday services is to expose more people, more souls to Christ's Way of Life and to the ministries of His church. This exposure is made acceptable by using approaches easily understood by the prospect. This strategy is like that of medical and agricultural missionaries who influence people by first appealing to an interest which is already part of their lives, and, then, after this bridge has been set up, use it to transmit new ideas.

Following is a discussion of some such special services. Church groups may think of others which would serve various needs.

FOUNDERS' DAY SUNDAY: Why not honor those families that founded your church? The Sunday nearest the official beginning of your congregation would be the best time. It's easy to build up a "Standing Room Only" congregation for this service. Personal letters go out to all living descendants of the founders, inviting them to attend Founders' Day Service. A section of seats in front of the church should be reserved for the Founders' families. This special service gives you the opportunity to have an *exhibit* of early church pictures in the vestibule or in the parish house. The more your congregation knows about the history of its church, the more interested and loyal it becomes. *Why wait for the fiftieth and seventy-fifth anniversaries of the church when you can celebrate Founders' Sunday every year?* Naturally, you will plan special music and an appropriate sermon for this special service.

Department stores have found that Founders' Day and Anniversaries are tested promotions for getting people to come into the stores. How much more worth-while it is to use these activating events to get people to attend services in your church.

GOOD NEIGHBOR SUNDAY: Here is a "natural" for practically every church. This special service stresses and takes advantage of that true Christian virtue—neighborliness. To Good-Neighbor Sunday service are invited all the people who live right around the church. A friendly letter carries the following invitation:

Dear Neighbor,

We, at (name of church) are proud of our neighbors. We believe your neighborhood and our neighborhood is one of the finest in the entire city.

This Sunday (date) we will have a special "Good Neighbor" service at 11 A.M. At that time, we will pay tribute to you and our other neighbors with special music and a special sermon.

If you have no church plans for this coming Sunday, we cordially invite you to join us in "Good Neighbor Sunday."

Sincerely yours,

(Hand-signed by minister)

MINISTER, NAME OF CHURCH

A notice should also go to the congregation. Here is suggested wording for a government post-card mailing to all members:

Dear Parishioner,

Sunday is "Good Neighbor Sunday" at (name of church). We honor your neighbors, and the church's neighbors.

The sermon pays tribute to good neighbors. Our fine choir will sing special music.

You will want to attend Good Neighbor Sunday at (name of church). So invite, and bring with you, some neighbor who does not attend any church regularly.

Yours faithfully,

NAME OF MINISTER

Notice that each invitation to neighbors is worded to attract those who do not attend any church regularly. Some church choirs are so informal they sing that lovely song, "Love Thy Neighbor."

As an extra attraction, you might collect and display in your vestibule pictures of your neighborhood in its early days. A picture committee would ask the congregation for exhibits. This feature exhibit should be mentioned in all announcements of the service. The local newspapers should be sent an advance publicity story on the service. An annual Good Neighbor Sunday is a proven way to increase church attendance and expose nonmembers to the comfort and inspiration of your services.

Good Neighbor Sunday is also an excellent opportunity for an annual combined service sponsored by a group of churches in the same neighborhood. It should be given on Sunday evening or during the week so it does not interfere with the regular Sunday services of the individual churches. The churches and ministers take turns in being hosts and preachers at this group service.

CHURCH SUNDAY SCHOOL: Each church should have at least two Sundays per year when the Sunday school attends the regular services —and takes part in the regular service.

BOY OR GIRL SCOUT SUNDAYS: These two services are growing in popularity and importance. Attending a special service in their honor, in their scout uniforms, makes an effective appeal to most boys and girls.

Properly planned and publicized, these services will attract attendance from the parents and families of scout members. The National Headquarters of both organizations usually designate a certain Sunday for these services. Front seats should be reserved for the scouts and their leaders. Having the church troop march in together is very effective.

A service in honor of the Campfire Girls is also worth-while.

MEDICAL SUNDAY: Why not have a special service to honor those men and women who keep people well, who help bring the sick back to health? Reserve the front pews for families of doctors or nurses. Send special letters of invitation to the heads of local hospitals and medical organizations. Ask them to send representatives to the service.

FLOWER SUNDAY: Hold a "Flower Sunday" in spring when due tribute is paid to God for His gift of flowers to our world. A special decoration committee would solicit donations of flowers and plants. These would be distributed to hospitals after the service.

MEMORIAL SERVICES: Some churches have an annual memorial service for families whose loved ones have died in the past year. This is a real comfort to the bereaved families, and assures attendance that Sunday from some who would otherwise not attend the service. The families can become a part of the service by contributing to the church flowers for that Sunday.

CHURCH DECORATION NIGHT: This is a beautiful service for some week-day night before Christmas. The congregation and neighbors are invited to decorate the church with Christmas greens. A Decoration Committee is formed to obtain the necessary material. Wire-screen forms and garlands are used as far as possible so that many amateur decorators can participate. The service starts at 7:00 P.M.; when the decorating is completed, a lighted star is raised and the choir (in regular week-day clothes) leads in singing "O Star of Wonder." This is followed by other familiar carols. The singing is closed with a prayer. Then all adjourn to the parish house where coffee and cookies are served.

GO-TO-CHURCH SUNDAY: Attendance at individual churches can be increased through a city-wide "Go-to-Church Sunday." Shown (p. 32) is

YOUR CHURCH IS CALLING

You!

"I am the best friend you ever had,
I am hung about with sweet memories . . .
Memories of friends . . . memories of mothers . . .
Memories of boys and girls . . . memories of angels.
I am blessed with loving thoughts . . .
Crowned by happy hands and hearts.
I safeguard man through all his paths.
I lift up the fallen. I strengthen the weak;
I help the distressed; I show mercy, bestow kindness, and
Offer a friendly hand.
I am good fellowship, friendliness and love.
Sometime . . . someday in the near or far future,
You will yearn for the touch of my friendly hand.
I am your comforter, and your best friend.
I am calling you now.
I AM YOUR CHURCH."

—Selected.

Heed this call in person! Lead the way for others!!

- The church represents the unseen "eternal lifting force" that is to save the world from destruction.
- The church through its leaders conceived and sponsored most of the great reforms. The social order of today is undergoing a change that challenges the church . . . the challenge to bring order out of chaos. Our children need this guidance and direction of the church to meet the situations they must face.
- Few human beings worship or labor alone. The church offers the strength of organization. It gives the urge of leadership, supplies encouragement when despondent, and offers rebuke when selfconfident.
- The church is the best place to share our abilities and resources. Presence is the evidence of accepted community responsibilities.

"To say that I do not need the church is mere bravado. I needed it when my father died. I needed it when we were married, and when our babies were taken from us, and I shall need it again sooner or later, and need it badly."

—Edgar A. Guest

CHURCH GOING FAMILIES ARE HAPPY FAMILIES!

Prepared by T. H. Stanley

the type of city-wide campaign material which can be used by all churches and produces good results. It was prepared by Mr. T. H. Stanley for the "Go-to-Church" Sunday in Columbus, Georgia, sponsored by the Junior Chamber of Commerce.

EDUCATIONAL SUNDAY: At this service, the church pays tribute to the fine work being done by the local school authorities and teachers. The date for this service is three or four weeks after school opens in the fall. It is best to arrange the exact Sunday with the principal of your neighborhood school. Explain the purpose of the service. Get from him the names and home addresses of his teachers and/or his entire staff. Show him the letter you plan to send these people, inviting them to the service. Plan to enclose a small but attractive card which introduces the recipient. This card enables the ushers to seat the school guests in the seats of honor, reserved for them at the front of the church.

Make sure your congregation is informed in advance of Educational Sunday. Urge them to attend and, by their presence, to honor the great contribution which the schools make to the training of youth. Suggest that their children ask the teachers to attend. Where possible, the members should phone and see if they can bring the teachers to church with them in their cars.

Churches that have this service report an unusual increase in attendance. As in the case of all special Sundays, some of the honored guests do not have a church affiliation. Therefore, a definite percentage of guests come back again and again to the church. And eventually some of them become regular members—active members.

LAYMEN'S SUNDAY: It is a known fact that most people take a greater interest in church attendance, and in Christ's Way of Life, when they are given special responsibilities. Thousands of churches of all denominations use "Laymen's Sunday" to build up this special interest on the part of key members, and to build up attendance on the third Sunday in October. In 1949 over 30,000 laymen spoke in their churches on "Laymen's Sunday." They discussed the application of Christian principles to everyday living and business affairs.

For a full outline on how to arrange a "Laymen's Sunday" in your church in connection with the national observance in October, write to: The Laymen's Movement for a Christian World, Room 1402, 347 Madison Avenue, New York 17, N.Y. You will be sent a free plan and all the necessary details.

NOTE ON GUEST CARDS: The success of all these special Sundays is increased when the letter of invitation includes a guest card of identification. It is possible to have these printed and filled in for the various occasions. Such a standard card can be as follows:

INTRODUCING OUR HONORED GUEST

....

(Name to be written on above line)

For whom a special place is reserved at our services on

....

(Date to be filled in)

Name of Church........................ Church Address........................

PLAN SHEET

Building Larger Congregations

Special Service	*Date of Service*	*Chairman in Charge*
Founders' Day	....	....
Good Neighbor Sunday	....	....
Church School Sunday	....	....
Medical Sunday	....	....
Flower Sunday	....	....
Girl Scout Sunday	....	....
Boy Scout Sunday	....	....
Campfire Girl Sunday	....	....
Educational Sunday	....	....
Go-to-Church Sunday	....	....
Laymen's Sunday	....	....
Church Decoration Night	....	....
Memorial Service	....	....
Other Special Sundays	....	....
LATE SLEEPER'S SUNDAY	....	....
GOLFER'S SUNDAY	....	....
NEW HAT SUNDAY	....	....
UNCLES' DAY	....	....
MASONS' VISITATION SUN.	....	....
*P.E.C. SUNDAY	....	....
PLEUTHNER R.I.P. SUNDAY	....	....
OLD CHESTNUT SUNDAY	....	....
REFORMATION SUNDAY	....	....
CIVIL DEFENSE SUNDAY.	....	....
WHITSUNDAY	....	....

WHAT ABOUT YOM KIPPUR?

* POSTMEN, FIREMAN & COPS'

8

Keeping the Away-at-School Crowd Going to Church

TO grow in size and influence, every church should have a continuing procession of boys and girls who will be future leaders in church activities. Some of these leaders should come from the youth who go away to school. It is tragic, but true, that colleges and out-of-town schools are not developing anywhere near their share of church leaders.

This is due to the fact that many boys and girls enter college with weak enough Christian convictions and entirely get out of the habit of going to church when they go away to schools. Many even lose their faith or become agnostics. No church can afford the loss of these potential leaders. When they come back home, their continued nonattendance is a serious influence on their contemporaries. Moreover, as more and more college-trained students assume most of the key positions in the industrial and professional worlds, their continued nonsupport of the church is a contributing factor to the financial difficulties and low salaries which afflict many churches today. Here are some ways to help prevent this happening to the away-at-school crowd of your church:

1. Find out the addresses of the boys and girls who are away at school. Then write the minister of a good church in each city. Most churches have annuals which list the college-school clergy. Ask him to call on the students and welcome them to the church services and activities. The home-town minister should also write the student and urge him or her to attend the school-town church.
2. Three or four times a year, send the students a copy of the church bulletin or some other news of their home-town church. In the accompanying letter, tell them you are looking forward to seeing them in church when they return for vacations.
3. Hold a tea or dinner for the away-at-school crowd during Christmas, Easter, or spring vacation.
4. Have a special service the first Sunday in September for students and their families.
5. Work with your denominational students' organization. The one I know best is the Church Society for College Work. You'll be encouraged and inspired by the fine job this organization is doing to keep school youth going to church, to help students keep and strengthen their faith, and to help local church groups better meet their school and college work. It brings leading ministers to school-town parishes. The Society helps provide funds to bring more and better chaplains into college centers. Like Army chaplains, college chaplains work among all groups. They provide friendship for the fearful, a mature guiding hand for the confused. They conduct chapel services, hold discussions on religion and present-day problems, and teach the Christian faith. They work closely with the college authorities and local ministers. They bring understanding and security to those who seek it.

This is not an experimental undertaking, but has been worked out successfully during the last ten years at Harvard University, Amherst College, University of North Carolina, Smith College, University of Wisconsin, and many other college centers.

Other denominations have similar organizations which concentrate their activities among schools. The names and addresses of some of these organizations are:

Church Society for College Work (Episcopal), Washington Cathedral, Mount St. Alban's, Washington, D.C.

The Westminster Fellowship (Presbyterian), Witherspoon Building, Philadelphia, Pa.

The Wesley Foundation (or Methodist Student Foundation), c/o The Board of Education, P.O. Box 871, Nashville, Tenn.

Student Service Commission (Lutheran), 77 West Washington Street, Room 719, Chicago, Ill.

PLAN SHEET

Keeping the Away-at-School Crowd Going to Church

1. *Getting Addresses of Out-of-Town Students*

   Chairman: ....

2. *Writing Letters to Ministers in School Cities*

   Chairman: ....

3. *Writing to Students Away at School*

   Chairman of Committee: ....

   Dates of Letters ....

4. *Sending Church Bulletins to Students*

   Dates When Bulletins Will be Sent:

   ....

   ....

5. *Holiday Social Functions for Students*

   Chairman: ....

   Date for Christmas Gathering ....

   Date for Easter Gathering ....

   Other Gatherings ....

6. *September Service for Students and Families*

   Chairman: ....

   Date ....

9

Building Attendance Through Better Singing

THERE is another way to increase church attendance which at first may seem of minor importance. Yet experience shows that improved congregational singing can improve the regularity of the attendance of existing members and even attract new members. This is because most people like to sing.

The singing at luncheon clubs, rallies, and social gatherings is evidence that most individuals enjoy being a part of the program. The ministry of music at any church is more effective when the congregation actually sings out instead of mumbling the words. Church services at which the members really participate in the singing give all a spiritual lift. For this lift, people will return again and again. It is one of the surest ways to make visitors feel at home in church and want to attend frequently.

Improved congregational singing is not dependent upon increasing the expenditures for the choir or organ. There are other successful methods which can be used by any church. Here are some of the most popular.

1. The best first step is to find out the favorite hymns of your congregation. The idea back of this is based on sound psychology. It lies in the fact that most adults like to sing the old familiar hymns they sang in childhood. They do not want to learn new hymns no matter how beautiful the choirmaster considers them. When people get together and sing in private homes or at service-club lunch meetings, or church-group get-togethers, they always go back to the old favorites. The radio "hit tunes of the week" are disregarded. Hymn singing is no different—the old familiar ones get the greatest response.

   It is very easy to determine which hymns your parishioners like to sing. All you do is put little mimeographed slips in the pews with the following request at the top—"Please write below the titles, first lines, or numbers of your favorite hymns." This simple survey form can also be included in your church bulletin. On the Sunday you make the survey be sure that pencils are put in the pews. Then make an explanatory announcement of the survey from the pulpit. Simply explain that you want to have the congregation's favorite hymns included in all Sunday services. In order to do this, you want to find out which hymns they like best. Then give the congregation five minutes to fill out their survey slips. The slips can be placed on the collection plate, collected separately, or left in the pews for collection after the service is over.

   Recently the Capitol Records people contacted several thousand churches throughout the country. Trained reporters asked the congregations to vote on their favorite hymns. Careful tabulations showed that twelve beloved hymns led all the rest. When you glance over the following titles, you'll agree these winners are a fine group for congregational singing:

   "Abide With Me"
   "For Thee, O Dear, Dear Country"
   "He Leadeth Me"
   "Holy, Holy, Holy"
   "Jesus, Lover of My Soul"

"Lead Kindly Light"
"Now the Day Is Over"
"O Love That Wilt Not Let Me Go"
"O Paradise"
"Onward Christian Soldiers"
"Saviour, Again to Thy Dear Name"
"The Church's One Foundation"

The above hymns are listed alphabetically, and not according to the voting of the congregations. All twelve have been recorded by the famous St. Luke's Choristers. This group needs little introduction as their voices are called upon by almost every motion-picture studio in Hollywood when church choir music is needed. Remember them in *Going My Way* and *Boys Town*?

This Capitol Album of Familiar Hymns should be owned by every church which has a phonograph. The records are excellent for your Young People's meetings. This album should also be in every home. For hymns are not just for Church on Sunday—they take on new meaning and increased beauty when brought to life in the home. Here are the old friendly hymns that the homemaker will enjoy on a quiet afternoon. Here, too, are the fine majestic hymns that will inspire the whole family in the cool of the evening. And what a lovely thought to have these masterpieces where growing youngsters can hear them often . . . learn to enjoy and love them in the old-fashioned way.

Other evidence on the relative popularity of different hymns was found in the fan mail received by the General Electric Company in connection with one of their Sunday radio programs. The radio audience was invited to vote for their favorite hymns. These favorites were high in the voting:

"Softly Now the Light of Day"
"Dear Lord and Father of Mankind"
"God Be with You Till We Meet Again"
"Love Divine"
"Eternal Father"

"Be Still My Soul"
"Faith of Our Fathers"
"Come Ye Thankful People Come"
"Rock of Ages"
"America the Beautiful"
"In the Garden"

No minister or choirmaster should ever worry about repeating the old favorites at frequent intervals. That's what congregations want and will respond to. If in your church, the ever-popular "Onward Christian Soldiers" is sung once a month, you'll get no complaints except possibly from the choirmaster or some professional singer. Please don't let that bother you. The basic objective of congregational singing is to get as many people as possible to join in the service with their voices. Experience shows there is nothing like old familiar hymns to inspire the congregation to sing out their praises, instead of mumbling through a beautiful but new song. To increase congregational singing, the St. Joseph of Arimathaea Church in Elmsford, N.Y. sings six hymns each Sunday.

2. One of the surest ways to increase singing and start the service on a high note of congregational participation, is to have the choir come down the main aisle singing the processional. This entrance always stimulates greater volume. It is not fair to either the choir or the congregation to have the choir enter from a door near the altar. To get the greatest inspiration, the processional should be sung as the choir proceeds through the congregation along the middle, main aisle.

Some churches are built so the choir cannot come down the center aisle during the winter. But in fair, warm weather, it is possible to have the assembled choir walk outside to the main door and then come down the main aisle singing the opening hymn.

Other churches have the choir come down the main aisle only at special services or on special Sundays. They admit this is a more effective processional but feel it should be reserved for special occasions. When any arrangement stimulates greater congregational singing, it should be used regularly.

3. The Christmas carols and Easter hymns include many of the favorite songs of churchgoers. Therefore they should be sung one or two Sundays preceding and following the day itself. Successful radio programs have found that Christmas carols are especially popular. So why shouldn't the Church which fathered the carols, offer this popular feature several times during the Christmas season?
4. Many churches have a Sunday school choir of boys and girls in addition to their adult choir. Where this is so, the youth choir should sing at the main service at least once every other month. Young voices are a delightful change and will attract increased attendance from friends, relatives, and neighbors.
5. Many churches make their procession more colorful and inspiring by including the church flag and the American flag.
6. The better the singing of the choir, the better the congregational singing. So here are two ways to stimulate your choir to even better singing:
   a. Once a year have a "Choir Sunday" at which the minister and church pay tribute to the fine support of the choir. Have front pews reserved for the families of choir members. Send out letters of invitation to all past and present families of choir members. Before the sermon, read a tribute to the choir and choirmaster.
   b. If you have a boy or girl choir, you have an unusual opportunity to show appreciation and stimulate even greater efforts. That is to provide crosses for the choir to wear at each church service. Silver crosses hung on red or purple ribbon make the choir feel more like a part of the church staff. Each boy or girl who has been in the choir one year or longer is given the right to wear the cross. This stimulates the new members to stay in and win their crosses at the end of the first year. When a member leaves the choir, he or she is presented with the cross as

a token of appreciation and as a remembrance of choir days. Presenting the crosses to the entire choir should be done at a special "Choir Sunday."

If the choir or church budget does not permit the purchase of crosses and ribbon, some leading member of the church will be willing to provide the funds. For instance, the choir crosses make an ideal gift in memory of a loved one. Sterling silver crosses measuring two and one-half inches long can be obtained for a low cost. The choir mothers can get the ribbon locally and sew 24 inches of ribbon on which to hang each cross.

7. Another scheme which works wonders with the young married group is to organize a volunteer choir from the young married women and their husbands for some series of Lenten or Advent services in the evening—this group to meet after work for a six-o'clock supper prepared by the group. The rector, the choirmaster, and the rector's wife are included. After supper the group rehearse simple music for an hour, then have a prayer, and march into church for the service. This gives the choirmaster an opportunity to teach the group how to sing properly. He explains what he is trying to do and the part real devotional music should have in the service. Here is the most important advantage. After the series is over, the choirmaster gets this group to scatter themselves around in the congregation at the regular services. Then they become focal points for good singing and bring their neighbors in the congregation into the habit of singing well and energetically.
8. A leading downtown church holds "congregation hymn practices" in connection with the regular service. Led by the choirmaster, these practices help the members sing the hymns better and easier. This plan is even more successful in a neighborhood church where the congregation is the same "family" each Sunday.

PLAN SHEET

Building Attendance Through Better Singing

1. Date of Survey on Favorite Hymns ....

2. Chairman of Survey Committee ....

3. Dates for Congregation Hymn Practice

   ....
   ....
   ....
   ....

4. Dates for Youth Choir at Regular Service

   ....
   ....

5. Date for Annual Choir Sunday ....

6. Possible Contributors of Crosses for Choir

   ....
   ....

7. Other Plans for Improving Congregational Singing

   ....
   ....
   ....
   ....
   ....
   ....

PART II

Increasing Financial Support

10

Preparing the Annual Appeal

THE need for greater support of the church and its activities is seen on every side of us. Mortgages are not paid off as promptly as they should be. Sunday schools do not have adequate equipment. Ministers are not paid enough to compensate for their ability, high calling, and continuous devotion to duty. Most important of all, too many churches receive so little support from their members that they cannot do their share of foreign and domestic missionary work. They are also unable to contribute their quota to the denomination's national organization.

Two other facts indicate the seriousness of this problem. The first is that only about 17% of all Americans have been sold on the plan for making an annual pledge of financial support. The rest are content to pay-as-they-attend or pay-as-they-use the various church services.

The second fact is the division of national expenditure expressed in the chart (page 50) made by the Golden Rule Foundation of New York.

These figures tell a story which should arouse every member of a church board. This comparison should be used in literature sent to members and used by canvassers. The churches can never fulfill their constructive mission on this earth *completely* until they are supported by expenditures which equal United States budgets for the Army and Navy.

WHERE DOES THE MONEY GO?

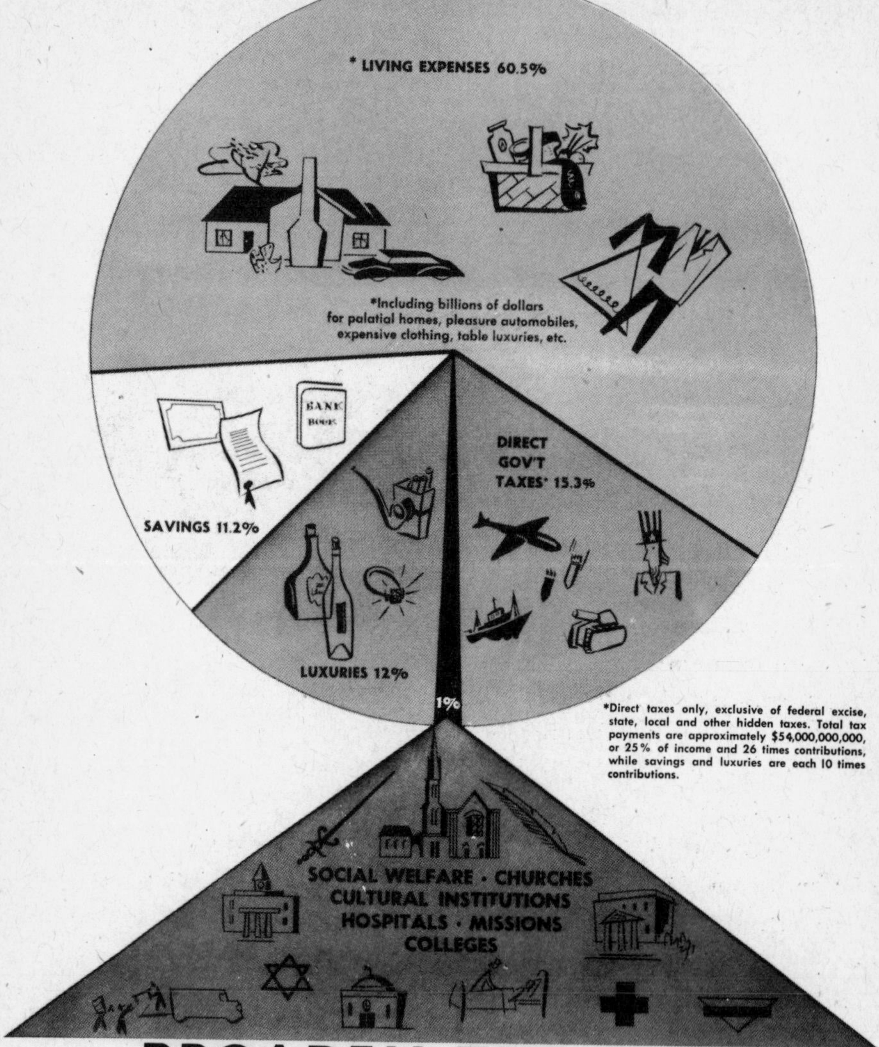

BROADEN THE BASE

Life, liberty and the pursuit of happiness, — and all other constitutional guarantees for the American way of life — depend upon those spiritual resources that flow from religious, cultural, social, and welfare organizations and institutions which in America as in no other nation, are dependent upon voluntary support for their maintenance. Such philanthropic giving now represents but one percent of the national income — ONE CENT OF THE AVAILABLE DOLLAR. We must BROADEN THE BASE to assure this more abundant life.

Golden Rule Foundation N. Y.

GRAPHICS INSTITUTE, NYC.

Here are tested ways which many churches have used to increase the support of their members at their annual financial appeal.

1. Prepare a report, in folder or letter form, on the services of the church during the past year. This report should include:

   a. Number of Services
   b. Number of Weddings
   c. Number of Funerals
   d. Number of Baptisms
   e. Number Who Joined the Church
   f. Total Annual Church Attendance
   g. Attendance at Sunday School
   h. Total Number of Contributors

   This same report should give a breakdown of where the past year's money was expended. This breakdown of expenditures should be done with simple diagrams, using either pie-charts or bar-charts. These take the place of a lengthy, wordy report which few people read or understand.

   The facts illustrated through pie-charts or bar-charts should include the following:

   Total Income..............................
   Pledges..............................
   Plate Collection..............................
   Donations from Organizations..............................
   Salaries..............................
   Amount of Endowment Fund..............................
   Report on Special Gifts..............................
   Money Spent in Domestic and Foreign Missions..........
   To National Denomination Headquarters ....

   Then you should outline the objectives of the coming year and how much money will be needed to carry them out. Some churches find it helpful to put down the average pledge for the past year, and what the average pledge should be in the coming year, in order to achieve the new financial goal. Then the can-

ESTIMATED INCOME OF TYPICAL CHURCH

Pledges	$14,150.00
Plate Collections	1,400.00
Special Collections	2,500.00
Miscellaneous	150.00
Legacies	500.00
	$18,700.00

ESTIMATED EXPENDITURES

Pastor's Salary	$4,300
Parish Office Workers	$2,968
Music	$2,320
Janitor, Treasurer	$2,170
Heat	$1,400
Printing, Publicity	$1,200
Share of Conferences	$1,100
Upkeep of Property	$700
Insurance	$600
Foreign Missions	$556
"Herald" and Calendar	$500
Electricity, Gas, Telephone	$450
Radio	$286
State Council	$150

vassers can urge "less-than-average supporters" to increase their pledges to an amount equal to the average or more, if possible.

At canvass time, put up a chart in the vestibule containing the figures on points a, f, g, and h.

A letter from the bishop or head of the church urging a generous support of the financial campaign is always helpful.

In developing this report, get the help of a member who has advertising or sales experience. He will know how to make the report more interesting and readable. He will use pictures if possible and will put effective selling into your appeal.

2. Appoint as head of your canvass committee a sales executive experienced in training and directing the efforts of salesmen.

   Mail the church report to members so it is received two or three days before the canvasser calls. In this report *first* thank the member for his past year's pledges. Point out that the church's record of service was made possible only through his support.

3. On the Sunday of your drive, have a prominent and well-liked member of the church give a ten-minute talk on the church's needs. In his talk, he should point out the church's opportunity to be of greater service to its members and to the community. He should ask the members to compare the amount of money they give to the church with the amount of money they spend for other activities including the following:

entertaining	movies and theatres
golf and social clubs	beauty parlors

   This should be graphically shown by taking total subscriptions in a year divided by total membership, divided in turn by fifty-two weeks. In most cases the amount will equal the price of a couple of popular magazines or less than the car fare to get to work.

   He could ask if the members were really proud of the amount they put down on their income tax as a church pledge, compared with the total amount of money received in salary and dividends.

4. Be sure that each pledge is acknowledged with a personal letter of thanks, signed by both the chairman of the drive and the minister. This helps develop "repeat pledges." Too many organizations only write the giver when pledges are due, and never write a "thank you" note.

Here is another example of a successful annual appeal. This "Every-Member Canvass" campaign was developed for the Congregational Church of Portland, Oregon. The creative and business programming of the soliciting was sparked by Lawrence A. Pierce, a top-flight sales executive, experienced in selling and motivating people.

Among the complete program of material were the following:

1. Opening the campaign with a government post-card mailing. This card carried the following message:

MEMBERS AND FRIENDS OF
FIRST CONGREGATIONAL CHURCH

PLEASE WATCH

for a letter, with enclosures, from the Division of Business relative to the Every-Member Canvass in behalf of the year's church budget! This should reach you next Monday.

SUNDAY, NOVEMBER 27TH

is Annual "Dedication Sunday" and you will, this year receive only ONE LETTER prior to the campaign for underwriting the year's expenses and benevolences. PLEASE READ THIS LETTER CAREFULLY AND HELP US MAKE THE CAMPAIGN A GREAT SUCCESS!

R. T. Titus, Chairman
Division of Business

2. The next mailing was a complete report and solicitation. It included a letter from "The Division of Business" (a good name for this part of church work), a fact folder, a stewardship folder, and a pledge card. Notice the splendid wording and tone of this letter.

To Members and Friends of First Church:

Sunday, November 27, is the IMPORTANT DAY when we underwrite the new budget of church expenses! It is always a happy day, for our people are enthusiastic about the Church. High-pressure, money-raising methods are out of keeping with the spirit of devotion and loyalty characteristic of First Church folk.

Again, this year, on "Dedication Sunday" we ask that pledges be brought or sent to the Church. In the Morning Service these will be collected and dedicated in a lovely ceremony. There will be no pulpit appeal for funds. There will be no pre-Dedication Sunday solicitation. This letter, with fact folder and pledge card, goes to all our people, presenting our needs. You are urged to give careful thought to your responsibility and privilege in sharing the underwriting of the forward moving program.

If you find it impossible to be present Sunday morning will you kindly mail your pledge to the Church office or send it by someone else so that you may be represented in the service of dedication AND SO THAT WE MAY QUICKLY COMPLETE OUR EVERY-MEMBER CANVASS. We do hope that you will be present.

The plan is very simple. People bring their pledges or send them on Dedication Sunday. Members of the Church from whom we do not hear, will be contacted personally as soon as possible after Dedication Sunday.

All pledges and contributions will be acknowledged by the treasurer and weekly payment envelopes provided those who desire these.

With appreciation for your co-operation in this important task.

Sincerely yours,

THE DIVISION OF BUSINESS

R. T. Titus, Chairman

The fact folder was an attractive, easy-to-read report with the title, "You and Your Church." The copy on the cover contained this line sure to step up reading:

READING TIME: 10 MINUTES

but please read it twice!

The most interesting section of this folder was the second page containing an interview with Mr. Titus, chairman. It read as follows:

A LITTLE TALK WITH MR. TITUS

YOU: Mr. Titus, may I ask you, as chairman of the Division of Business of our Church, for a few facts? How much is the 1950 budget?

MR. TITUS: $39,045.00. See the next page for a breakdown of this total. $30,270.00 must be obtained in gifts and pledges from individuals; other sources of income care for the balance.

YOU: Does the $39,045.00 include benevolences?

MR. TITUS: It does. We have set $9,050.00 as our share in the wider Christian program, and $8,000.00 of this is for the "Christian World Mission" of our own denomination.

YOU: How was the budget prepared and who set the amounts?

MR. TITUS: The Executive Council, consisting of officers and division heads, received "askings" from the various departments, co-ordinated these into a budget and recommended the same to the Church at a special meeting —a very democratic procedure.

YOU: What is MY share of the $30,270.00 to be raised in pledges?

MR. TITUS: Well, that is for YOU to say! Giving should be part of one's religious experience, a matter for careful thought and prayer. The amount should be determined by one's own ability to give, not by what others do or do not do.

YOU: Well, what is the AVERAGE contribution?

MR. TITUS: 1949 pledges, not counting children, number 492 with a total of $25,767.00, an average of approximately $52.00 or $1.00 per week. But if no one gave more than the average, of course, the budget would never be raised! Many cannot afford to give that much.

YOU: Is the budget larger for 1950?

MR. TITUS: Yes, and we are proud to say: the largest in First Church history! To cover it we must have more people giving and people giving more. We shall need approximately $5,000 in new money.

YOU: That's an increase of 20% in pledges. Can we get it?

MR. TITUS: Surely! There are few of us who couldn't give more than we do.

YOU: What of people who, because of uncertain income, feel that they cannot pledge a specific amount?

MR. TITUS: They can pledge a percentage of their income—whatever it may be. The Bible tithe is 10% but most of us give much less.

YOU: On what basis are pledges made?

MR. TITUS: Most people pledge an amount WEEKLY, others monthly or quarterly and some give a lump sum. Weekly or monthly payments mean a stabilized income for the Church, but terms of payment are always left to each individual.

YOU: What are the plans for underwriting the budget?

MR. TITUS: Please read our letter regarding the Every-Member Canvass. A copy is enclosed.

This folder, like any good direct mail piece, was printed in an attractive color. It was printed in brown on a canary yellow paper stock. Too many church mailings are always black, the color of mourning.

The stewardship folder enclosed was "Givers are Likest God." It was obtained from the Commission on Stewardship and the Missions Council at 287 Fourth Avenue, New York (10), New York.

11

Loyalty Sunday, A Stimulus to Generous Support

THE newest and most successful plan for increasing church support is "Loyalty Sunday." This is a method developed and perfected by Austin Pardue, now Bishop of the Pittsburgh diocese of the Episcopal Church. He discovered that most churchgoers would rather express their loyalty by pledging at church in their pews than waiting at home until a canvasser called. In addition, Loyalty Sunday always results in pledges from people who attend the church more or less regularly but are not listed on the rolls as members.

Records prove that pledging in church is more conducive to increased contributions than canvassers calling at the home, for the nearness to God felt in church is not usually equalled in the home. Pledges signed in church can be gathered by the ushers, presented on plates to the minister, and then blessed by him at the altar. Funds devoted to God's work are so important they should be consecrated to God's work in front of the givers.

A well-filled church on Loyalty Sunday is a great stimulus to generous support. In itself, it develops loyalty and increases the congregation's pride in the parish.

Another big advantage of Loyalty Sunday is the saving of time. Canvassers do not have to call on loyal members who pledge in their pews. Letters mailed to all members the week before Loyalty Sunday increase attendance and thus reduce the follow-up calls. In the advance letter, the member is given a report of the church's work for the past year (see page 52). Here is a letter used by Bishop Edward R. Welles of St. Paul's in Buffalo, New York, when he was Dean.

Dear Mr. and Mrs. . . . . (hand-written by the Dean)

You and I belong to a church with a great spirit of loyalty and service. For 128 years St. Paul's has loyally served God and man at the very heart of this growing city. During all those years loyal men and women have given gladly to make that service possible.

Today St. Paul's stands open and accessible to the thousands who come to worship, to be quiet, and to seek personal help. They come from every walk of life, every part of the city and the world, every race and creed and color and age. They do not come in vain.

In a very real sense the Cathedral serves two congregations: the whole community, including transients; and the 3,704 persons on our parish list. For the latter group, St. Paul's provides additional strength and inspiration by hundreds of pastoral calls on regular members and newcomers, on the sick, the shut-in, and the bereaved—and by Christian education in the largest Episcopal Sunday School in western New York.

Loyalty Sunday will be held on November 19th. Make every necessary sacrifice to be present and to pledge on faith for the new budget. In due proportion to your faith you will be blessed.

A year ago not a single home solicitation was necessary. In my first year as your Dean, I am counting on you to back me to the hilt. I need the power of your prayers, your presence, and your pledges.

Come and make November 19th a real Loyalty Sunday!

Affectionately yours,

(Signature hand-signed)

The church bulletin for St. Paul's on Loyalty Sunday carried the following message:

OFF THE MINISTER'S DESK

Once again we come to a high spot in our year at St. Paul's—Loyalty Sunday. It is truly a high spot because it is our annual opportunity to express in a tangible financial fashion our deep sense of loyalty to St. Paul's and to Almighty God and the work of His church throughout the whole world. We have the chance to come and offer in the privacy of our pew. There is an extra satisfaction, it seems to me, in being able to give voluntarily and freely, without the pressure of a personal solicitation.

May I make three suggestions for your expression of loyalty? First, offer the maximum when you fill in your pledge card. Second, do it on faith. Don't hold back through fear of what may happen in the future—you will be blessed in proportion to your faith, and remember that any pledge made to St. Paul's may be changed (either increased or decreased) at any time by giving notice to the treasurer. Third, if you are ill or out of town and cannot come to the Loyalty service, please let me know immediately, so that I may send you a pledge card and return envelope for your convenience in sending in your pledge by mail.

THIS IS LOYALTY SUNDAY—COME AND OFFER

At the service on the week following Loyalty Sunday, members or guests who did not attend the preceding Sunday are given an opportunity to pledge. Then the remaining members who have not pledged are contacted personally by canvassers. Loyalty Sunday reduces the job of canvassing by 70 to 90%. It is a proven method of increasing pledges and getting new additional pledges. It merits a trial in nearly every church.

As a personal build-up to the church's pledge-making Sunday, the Reverend Robert W. Anthony (Minister of the North Presbyterian Church, Flushing, Long Island, New York), staged a most successful telephone roll call of the entire parish. One Saturday at 10 A.M., he sat down with a list of phone numbers of every member.

During each call, he told the family about the special talk which would be given at the Sunday service by Philip Everest. He explained that this leading layman, a member of another congregation, was going to talk on the subject of church finances and church support. At 5:30 P.M., the Reverend Anthony stopped, worn out by constant phoning and talking. The reward was apparent the very next day when the church had a "Standing Room Only" congregation. As a result of the unusual turnout, plus Mr. Everest's talk, and the great loyalty of North Church members, pledges for church support were tripled and pledges for benevolences were quadrupled. So, when planning a Loyalty Sunday, don't forget the effectiveness of phone calls by the clergy and lay workers. The build-up and persuasiveness of the human voice are hard to equal.

The canvassers of the North Presbyterian Church say that they were helped by the excellent "Turnover" presentation prepared for the Presbyterian Church by the Jam Handy Organization of Detroit, Michigan. Other churches could use this businesslike presentation to good advantage.

A "Turnover" presentation is a modern, successful way of selling ideas, merchandise, and even organizations to prospective customers. It is a loose-leaf binder of "selling" pages which, when open, sets up like a pyramid. Each page is turned over, from front to back, of the pyramid-hinged top. Each page carries a separate selling idea or message. These ideas flow logically to a conclusion page which requests the "audience" to do something. Thus the user of a Turnover presentation has the advantage of a planned, pretested interview. A Turnover on church support helps make the average volunteer a better salesman and solicitor. The pages can be almost any size. While these Turnovers cost a little money, they can pay for their costs in a greater number of increased pledges.

12

Tithing, the Oldest and Surest Method

THE perfect way to support one's church is to go back to the Bible plan of "tithing." Giving one-tenth of one's salary or income for Christ's work in this world is the surest method of giving your church the support it deserves and should have. For years people said it couldn't be done—it wouldn't leave enough money in the budget for the family to live on. Yet during the recent years of steadily increasing taxes, millions of families have been "tithing in taxes." These families still have enough left for living expenses. The well-to-do families are now paying taxes which are many times more than 10% of their income.

Just think what would have been accomplished before the establishment of our high tax set-up if churchgoers had tithed! Think of the settlement work, the social service jobs, the free health clinics, the home and foreign missionary activities which could have been carried out.

Is "tithing" an ideal which is impossible in these unsettled times? Ed Davidson of the Rose Hill Methodist Church in Columbus, Georgia, will answer you NO. He has revived that Biblical plan of pledging and the number of tithers in his church is growing every month. Many people who are "tithing for taxes" can be sold on "tithing for Christ." Remember that tithers do not have to earn more money than others.

They learn to budget and spend their remaining income wisely. In return, the tithers have the satisfaction of knowing they are true Christian stewards of Christ's gifts to them.

You can obtain some excellent statistics, arguments, and charts for your yearly pledge campaigns by writing to the National Stewardship Institute of The Golden Rule Foundation. The objective of this Institute is to help churches, colleges, hospitals, and other privately supported welfare agencies to obtain increased financial and moral support commensurate with our increased national wealth, higher living standards, and unprecedented opportunities and obligations.

The Institute has prepared a complete plan for increasing the individual's support of churches and charities. Its material is so helpful, its suggested appeals so effective, that you should write for full information before preparing your material for any money-raising campaign. Their offices are located as follows:

National Headquarters:	60 East 42nd Street, New York 17, New York, Charles V. Vickrey
Midwestern Office:	1 North LaSalle Street, Chicago, Illinois, C. F. Jackman
Pacific Coast Office:	1 Drum Street, San Francisco, California, Fred D. Parr
Southern California:	606 South Hill Street, Los Angeles, California, Clarence W. Horn
Southern States area:	Travelers Building, Richmond, Virginia, Hill Montague

13

Reselling a Church to Its Members

WHEN the Reverend William Kirk went to St. John's Church in Buffalo, New York, he assumed spiritual leadership of a parish which was about to celebrate its 100th anniversary. Instead of having just the usual centennial celebration, the St. John's board decided to include one continuing basic objective in their anniversary plans. That was to embark on a campaign to resell St. John's to its members and friends.

To do this, a series of letters was written by a successful insurance salesman. Here are some of the letters. They are well worth editing and adopting by other churches. Thanks to the low cost of direct mail, these letters are an economical way to build up enthusiasm, interest, and loyalty.

Says a Layman to a Layman:

A CHURCH FOR SALE

Dear Member,

It may be news to you but as indicated by the caption we are going to sell St. John's Church. At least, we are going to try.

We are going to sell the grounds, the building, the traditions, the services, the choir and, yes, even the bell.

If this statement has caused you to feel a little twinge of regret somewhere down deep within you—don't let it, because we are going to sell St. John's Church to you.

This letter is not intended for those loyal men and women and young people of our church who for many years have given generously of their time and effort, but is primarily intended for members such as I, who, year in and year out, have taken the church for granted and have done so little to help those who have worked so hard.

We go to church on Easter come hell or high water and again we grace the pews at Christmas (because we like the carols) and we sing lustily and we put a dollar in the collection plate and we go home feeling quite content now that we have discharged our duties to the church and Christianity for another year.

Oh yes, it's true we sign a pledge card when called upon during the "Every-Member Canvass," usually for an amount much less than we should (and we know it) and it's true that when some hard-working member calls us on the telephone and asks us to be present "Please" on Loyalty Sunday or some other special occasion we do, at great sacrifice of personal comfort, bestir ourselves.

It is to this group, of which I blushingly admit I am one, that this letter and those which follow are addressed in the hope that we can sell St. John's Church to you.

Please file this letter as there are several more to come. When the series is completed, I will ask you to read each one through just once more, beginning with the first and continuing to the last without interruption. After that it will be up to you to show whether we have been successful in selling you St. John's Church, the grounds, the building, the traditions, the services, the choirs, and, yes, even the bell.

Sincerely yours,

John Greeno
(hand-signed)

A CHURCH FOR SALE

The Ground, The Buildings, The Traditions

Dear Member,

One hundred years ago, a few churchmen among the early settlers of Buffalo, recognizing the need of a place of worship in what was at that time not much more than a frontier village, got together and organized St. John's Church.

This was no easy task. In those days money was scarce and members were few. One dollar represented a hard day's work—and it took many dollars to buy the land and erect a building that would be suitable as a place where this group of churchmen and their families could gather on Sunday morning and hold services.

Little wonder then that it was a proud and happy day when the first spade full of earth was turned and the project began. Little wonder that it was an even happier and prouder day when the first service was held within its walls.

That was one hundred years ago.

These were men and women of vision and foresight, with no fear of what the future might have in store for them. St. John's Church grew and served its community faithfully and well.

I will not dwell longer on the history of St. John's Church as that history has been written by a far more capable person than I, but looking back down the years we can now see what the "future" held in store for that brave little group. The war between the states, the panic of '93, the plagues and epidemics of the late '90s and the financial crashes of 1907 and 1929, just to name a few.

These problems were met in turn as they arose and St. John's was skillfully guided through these shoals and continued to wield its kindly and beneficent influence on mankind.

Today, we, you and I, are the successors to that same little band of churchmen whose early efforts have given us our opportunity to serve. We are the direct beneficiaries of all that has been done by them. We find ourselves the proud owners of a church building which is a gem of architecture, all built and paid for; but, if that were all we had, we would be poor indeed. Our riches lie in that wealth of experience, tradition, and the example of self-sacrifice which has been handed down to us by those who have gone before. The history of St. John's Church is our inspiration and the future of St. John's Church will be what we make it.

We will have many problems to face during the years of our custodianship. So will those who follow us.

Let us then take a page from the book of our predecessors and look to the future with confidence. Let us be sure that when younger hands take the helm, the good ship, St. John's Church, will be just as sturdy a craft to sail the seas of the uncertainties of tomorrow as it was when we took over.

The only way to be sure of this is to keep our crew pulling together, to avoid dissention in the ranks—to rise above the many little things that annoy us and at all cost avoid letting our group split into factions.

After all, we are the Church. If there is work to be done, we should do it. If there is any credit to be gained by a job well done, we should do it. If there is any blame for the way things are done, we should be blamed.

There are bound to be differences of opinion on the way things are done or why they are done; but, if we keep firmly in our minds the fact that "The Church" is NOT THE BUILDING, NOT THE RECTOR, NOT THE VESTRY, but all of us, each and every one of us, individually and collectively, then we will find a way to adjust our differences of opinion and work together for the common good.

Remember WE ARE THE CHURCH and when we say this or that is wrong with "The Church" what we are really saying is, this or that is wrong with US.

Let's just give this idea a tryout and see if it doesn't give us a little broader perspective and help us to work together to the end that St. John's Church will be able to take a more prominent part in the development of our community.

Sincerely yours,

JOHN GREENO
(hand-signed)

A CHURCH FOR SALE

The Services, The Choir, The Bell

Dear Member,

The services of St. John's Church—am I about to tread heavily on some thin ice?—perhaps, but here goes anyway. Let's kick it around a bit. It will do us good no matter what we think.

Let's start this way: When you read the first line of this letter, did you think of the "Morning Service" held at eleven o'clock on Sunday, or did you think of the term in its broader sense which includes ALL of the MANY services rendered by the Church?

For example, did you think of that all-important service of organizing and maintaining an efficient staff for the religious education of our children, the Church School?

Did you think of the baptism of our babies, the confirmation of our youngsters, the marriage of our young people, and the accurate records that must be kept of all these events?

If you did, fine, for those and many others are the services that we so often overlook.

St. John's Church has always stood high on the lists for its accomplishments both at home and abroad.

Never have the people of St. John's failed to hold up their end in any church activity, and I am sure we can all be justly proud of what has been done in the past.

We want to be equally proud of what we will do in the future, but a church cannot stand still. If we are to be proud of what we do in the future, then, we must plan for the future. If we plan for the future, we must back up our plans with the necessary money to see them through.

A tree stems from roots planted firmly in the ground. The services we hope to render through our parish must stem from our church planted in our community.

If our financial structure is weak, then our plans will collapse; but if we do, as we have always done, look our problems squarely in the face, and back our plans with our money, then St. John's

Church will go forward to greater heights of accomplishments and be in fact the spiritual POWER we all hope and pray for.

Next Sunday, as has been announced, will be LOYALTY SUNDAY. The choir has worked to have a special program of music for this occasion. The warm and friendly chime of St. John's bell which has rung down through the years will bid you WELCOME as you approach the outer doors.

It is on this day that by our presence we demonstrate to our church, to ourselves, and to each other our determination to support St. John's Church and all it stands for.

It is on this day that you will show, by your presence, whether we have been successful in SELLING ST. JOHN'S CHURCH to you, including the grounds, the buildings, the traditions, the services, the choir, and, yes, even the bell.

Sincerely yours,

JOHN GREENO
(hand-signed)

Results of the letters from St. John's

The Reverend Mr. Kirk reports that these three letters were a major factor in obtaining pledges totaling almost 15% higher than the previous year. Equally important was the fact that many brand new givers responded and pledged for the first time.

PLAN SHEET

Increasing Financial Support

1. *Amount Pledged* ....

   Amount Paid ....

Year	*Total Amount*	*Gain or Loss over Previous Year*
19	....	....
19	....	....
19	....	....
19	....	....

2. *Average Contribution*

	Average Pledge or Paid	*Comparison with Year Before*
19	....	....
19	....	....
19	....	....
19	....	....

3. *Plans to Increase Pledges*
   Loyalty Sunday Program

Date ....

Chairman ....

Committee Members

....

....

....

4. *People to Work on Booklet,* Letters, and Other Announcements

....

....

....

....

....

....

....

5. *Ideas for Thank-you Letter*

....

....

....

....

....

6. *Other Ideas for Building Church Support*

....

....

....

....

....

....

7. *Material for Which to Send*

....

....

....

PART

III

Publicizing Your Church

14

Use a Basic Theme

by Alex F. Osborn

A FRIEND recently startled me by asking: "Just why do you go to church?" We had long worked together, both in business and as social-service volunteers. I knew his curiosity to be sincere. So I told him, "I go to church because it makes me feel better." He thought a minute, then let me off with, "Well, it's a bit fuzzy, but even so, it's as good a reason as I have heard."

Millions of splendid men and women are as puzzled about church-going as he is. The nation's two hundred and fifty thousand churches have over seventy-nine million members, and yet, never, except on Easter, do more than thirty-eight millions of us go to church.

"What of it?" many a nonchurchgoer will ask. "What good will it do to try to get us to go to church? We don't need the church any more. The school has taken its place."

But is that so? Can the onrush of education make up for the stand-still of religion? Was H. G. Wells right in saying that civilization is a race between education and catastrophe? Or was George Washington right when he said, "Whatever can be conceded to be the influence of education, national morality cannot prevail in exclusion of religious principles." Educators like Dr. Robert M. Hutchins, Chancellor of the University of Chicago, agree with Washington. "Schools cannot take the place of the church," said Dr. Hutchins in a recent writing. And even arch-scientists agree with Dr. Hutchins. In "Man the Unknown,"

Dr. Alexis Carrel wrote this: "Moral sense is more important than intelligence. When it disappears from a nation, the whole social structure slowly commences to crumble away."

More and more businessmen are realizing that churchgoing is the lifeblood of our civilization. Colonel Samuel W. Fleming, Jr. told the Chamber of Commerce in Harrisburg: "A sympathetic interest in the church may be the fundamental solution of our national difficulties." Donald Adams recently put it this way: "A keen spiritual hunger stirs in the world. It leads men in other countries to accept baser equivalents in the form of dictators' calls—*we* must find our own faith or perish as free men."

Yes, to go or not to go to church is a truly vital question. And yet nothing is being done about it, nothing compared with what we do to cure cancer, or to support the Red Cross, or to get votes.

What can be done? "Nothing," a lot of intelligent stay-aways will say. "We don't like church as it now is. Make churchgoing more attractive and we will go." Toward that attitude, many true friends of the church will feel some sympathy. They will admit its sermons, its music—yes, its showmanship—could be bettered. But they know it takes time to improve an institution as old and as successful as religion. Lifelong loyalties of millions of devotees stand in the way of any speedy program of streamlining. And anyway, isn't today's model right enough so that it *should* attract a far greater part of the public? It is an axiom of business that if anything is good enough to win its way without advertising, it can win its way a lot further if it is advertised. And the church as it now is, proves itself good enough to attract thirty million fairly steady churchgoers. Churchgoing is about the only thing these millions do without persuasion of some kind.

When churches use the basic theme on their outside bulletin board, they remind thousands of people every day about the true happiness which comes only from churchgoing. This right-angle position for a bulletin board assures more readership than when the bulletin is parallel to the sidewalk. →

"Church Going Families
are
Happier Families"
Henry C. Link

To fill more pews, we must find the right appeal and then propel that appeal. The right appeal must be based on the simplest, the most moving reason why so many millions of us *do* go to church. In our search for this key, we must tear tradition from our eyes. We must see that appeals to duty will not do. To say: "You ought to go to church—otherwise the nation will go to the bow-wows," would be as futile as if General Motors were to say: "You ought to buy our cars because we pay over $250,000,000 a year for taxes."

My business partner, Bruce Barton, once wrote: "Unless business holds steadily before its eye a spiritual ideal, unless the Church learns some of the lessons that business has been forced to learn under keenly competitive conditions, neither will measure up to its opportunities." Practicality is the first lesson the church can learn from business. This means that any churchgoing appeal must be pragmatic. It should dodge the doubts that keep so many away. I know these doubts. I never would have joined a church had not my minister confessed that even he had doubts. I still have them but they have been largely erased by the feeling that churchgoing really *works* and, as William James said, "That which works is true!"!!!?

Let's find out first what is the most wanted thing that the Church can offer. Dr. W. Russell Bowie, former rector of New York's Grace Church, states a minister's view: "Without ideals, life is mean. Without a purpose, it is flat. Without inspiring power, it will fail. The Church gives men ideals, purpose, power."

"Ideals, purpose, and power,"—do they add up to anything that everybody wants, such as happiness, for instance? Dr. Henry C. Link summed up his ideas in this way: "The findings of psychology are largely a rediscovery of old religious truths . . . individuals who believe in religion or attend a church have significantly better personalities than those who do not. . . . My reason for attending church again is that I have recommended it to so many others," Another outstanding psychologist, Dr. Carl Jung, says the same thing in these words: "Among all my patients over thirty-five, there has not been one whose problem in the last resort was not that of finding a religious outlook on life. It is safe to say that every one of them fell ill because they had lost that which the living religions of every age have given to their followers. Not one of them has been really healed who did not regain his religious outlook."

Roger Babson has packed into one simple sentence his selfish reason for going to church: "I enjoy my church as I enjoy my daily walk." A physician, writing in *The Forum* puts the same thought backward: "For a good many years I have stayed away from church. Quite recently, however, I decided to return. I realize now that I was *unhappy* outside the church."

A churchgoing appeal should meet this basic test of successful advertising: "Does your message tell the reader what he will get out of what you offer?" In other words, the appeal must fit in with human *desires*. Envy is one of these desires and is often used in mass-persuasion. For instance: boys would ape world champions. Based on that appeal, wheat flakes have been put on millions of tables where corn flakes used to be. Other basic desires include pride, profit, fear, and fun.

Appeals based on self-interest dig deep because human nature is selfish. Even Christ admitted that, when He said: "Thou shalt love thy neighbor as thyself." But selfishness need not be ignoble. It often embraces more than one's self. Love of offspring, love of country—both are partly selfish. Right living is impossible without love of self. Even preaching is seldom selfless.

The nerve center of selfishness varies. Mothers can be moved by child-appeals. Unmarried women usually cannot be so moved to the same extent. Peoples-at-war can be moved by patriotic appeals. A people-at-peace can't. The strongest of all self-interest is group loyalty *plus* individual selfishness. These two instincts are joined in family happiness. Few are free from such self-interest. Even adolescents dream fondly of their families-to-be. And childless couples, though far beyond the spell of romance, still long for family happiness. There are many proofs that this is an Achilles' heel, vulnerable to religion. When home ties tug as hard as they do at times of birth, marriage, or death, this urge wells up and the Church is then invited into unchurched homes.

Yes, the Church is one answer, perhaps *the* answer, to mankind's longing for family happiness. From every angle, *family happiness* seems to be the human desire around which a churchgoing appeal could best be built. But how could such an appeal be wrapped into a small package? Here is one way . . . in these five homely words: CHURCH-GOING FAMILIES ARE HAPPIER FAMILIES. Such a claim would be positive. Surely it could be made as powerful as other slogans such as "Schoolgirl Complexion," "Do as your dentist does," "Say it with flowers," "Don't write, telegraph," or "Not a cough in a carload."

But—wait. Before entering on campaigns, modern advertisers insist that the basic idea be checked. They no longer take the verdict of logic, or the word of the expert. To do away with much of the old-time guess-

THE SCARSDALE INQUIRER, SCARSDALE, NEW YORK

Church News of the Week

"CHURCH-GOING FAMILIES ARE HAPPIER FAMILIES"

Christian Science
Post and Drake Roads

Sunday School at 9:30; Sunday services at 11 and five. Wednesday evening meetings at 8:15. Reading Room, 4 Spencer Place, open week days and Saturdays, except holidays, 10 to five.

"Love" is the Lesson-Sermon subject for Sunday. Golden Text: "The Lord hath appeared of old unto me, saying, Yea, I have loved thee with an everlasting love: therefore with loving-kindness have I drawn thee'" (Jeremiah 31:3). Sermon: From the King James version of the Bible (I John 4: 12,13,16). Correlative passages from "Science and Health with Key to the Scriptures" will be

Climate of Our Age" with Fred Judy, leader.

Monday, board of deacons and deaconesses, 8:15. Tuesday, all-day meeting of sewing group of Woman's Society, 10 to four. Wednesday, Mercer Club, 8:30, with manager of a chain store speaking on the problems of a manager.

+

Greenville Community Church
Central Avenue at Old Army Road

Church School, 9:30. Church worship service, 11, with observance of Youth Sunday, the service being conducted by members of the Youth Fellowship and an address by Dr. Donald T. Bosch, a

Redeemer Lutheran Church
Murray Hill and Post Roads

Church School, 9:30. Worship service, 11, with sermon by the Rev. Edwin H. Lehr. Nursery for children two to eight years every Sunday morning during 11 a.m. service.

+

Religious Society of Friends
Popham Road

Meeting for worship and First Day School, eleven a.m.

+

St. Andrew's Church
Columbia Avenue, Hartsdale

Church School, 9:30 a.m. Morning service, eleven a.m.; vicar, the Rev. Dr. Percy L. Johnson.

+

St. James the Less

Here is how one newspaper uses the basic theme, or slogan, in its masthead for the church page. You should sell the editor in chief, or religious editor, of your local paper on similar use of "Churchgoing Families Are Happier Families."

work and desk-pounding, they first find out from enough people just why those people buy whatever they seek to sell. The *American Magazine* has made such a survey. Its editors prompted over 7,000 readers to write in and state just why they go to church. These letters confirm the fact that the combination of individual and family happiness looms up above all other reasons for churchgoing.

Intelligent planning also calls for a critical analysis of the resistance that must be met. In selling almost anything, the seller is up against both cost *and* habit. In persuading people to go to church, purse resistance would be almost nil. The redirecting of habit would be the chief task. Dr. Albert G. Butzer found this to be so when minister at Ridgewood, New Jersey. On questionnairing citizens as to why they didn't attend church, he listed ten possible reasons. The reason indicated by the great majority was this: "Just got out of the habit." Next came: "Household duties." Third came the claim, "We go to church at home via radio."

It is likely that church prospects may be more receptive than some of us might expect. This fact was recently indicated when a businessman in New York was asked whether he went to church. He replied: "The last time I went to church was two years ago when my mother died. If we had children, we would send them to Sunday school. I wish I *wanted* to go regularly." There are probably fifty million people like him—people who *would* go to church if they could be made to feel it would do them enough good.

Granted a sound appeal, how could it be propelled? Probably by the same forces which have changed so many other habits—have led women to use three creams on their faces—have led boys to gather box tops—have led men to switch from dental powder to tooth paste and then back again to dental powder. Nearly all these forces could be put behind churchgoing at a fraction of what they would cost a commercial advertiser.

With wholehearted, united effort, the possibilities challenge the imagination. In the average city, a few thousand dollars, plus countless hours of volunteer effort, could develop an unprecedented power. Done as it could be done, this drive could equal or eclipse any other appeal, commercial or civic, that the community had ever known. All told, if the nation's 200 urban areas were to generate similar power, the aggregate would roll up into a national force that no commercial advertiser could buy for less than $10,000,000 a year. And that is an understatement.

PLAN SHEET

Publicizing the Basic Theme

"Churchgoing Families are Happier Families"
(or other basic theme)

People to notify and things to do in order that the above theme be included in the following:

1. On Outside Church Bulletin Board

   ....
   ....
   ....

2. On Printed Weekly Church Bulletin

   ....
   ....
   ....
   ....
   ....

3. On Inside Church Bulletin Board

   ....
   ....
   ....

4. On Individual Boxes for Pledge Envelopes

   ....
   ....
   ....

5. At Bottom of Church Letterheads

   ....
   ....
   ....

6. On Outside Church Identification Name Plate

   ....
   ....
   ....

7. Painted on Wall of Main Sunday School Room

   ....
   ....
   ....
   ....
   ....

8. Added to Base of Church Advertisements When Space Permits

   ....
   ....
   ....

9. Included in Sermons Whenever Logical and Possible

   ....
   ....
   ....

15

"Support Your Church" Newspaper Evangelism

A REGULAR program of properly planned publicity can help a church attract visitors and in the end obtain new members. It is also a sure way to increase attendance from the regular congregation. Church publicity reminds the reader of an institution which warrants attendance and support. It reminds us about the greatest source of true happiness.

Each church should have a publicity committee. On that committee you should have at least one person experienced in writing items for newspapers. If possible, have an advertising man or woman on that committee. They know what is significant and how to publicize it.

The publicity committee sees to it that a publicity story on important church events is written and sent to the local paper. Someone from the committee should meet the local newspaper editors to whom news stories are sent.

In sending publicity items to local papers, be sure each story answers the "five famous news questions":

1. WHO?
2. WHAT?
3. WHEN?
4. WHERE?
5. HOW?

Here are some of the events which warrant a good publicity story:

Start of Sunday School Year
Graduations from School
Confirmation Sunday
Special Speaker at Men's Club Meeting
Election of Church Officers
Election of Organization Officers
Special Sunday Services
Twenty-fifth, Fiftieth, or Seventy-fifth Anniversary
of Founding of Church
Appointment of New Organist or Choirmaster
Burning of Mortgage or Paying Off Loan
Unusual Gifts Like Stained-Glass Windows
Christmas and Easter Music

Here is a way to assure that the members of your congregation, and prospective members, will see more religious articles, stories, and editorials in their favorite publications. The way is simple and proved. All you do is write to the editor and express your appreciation of the religious material which he published in his newspaper or magazine. His name and address can always be found in the official masthead of the publication.

It is a fact that when an editor gets fine letters of appreciation, he will continue to use religious material. This encouragement is the responsibility of clergy and laymen. If your local newspapers carry a daily meditation, bible quotation, or weekly sermon, send a "thank you" note to the editors. At some time you could write the editors of *Time, Newsweek,* and *Quick* magazines expressing your appreciation of their weekly editorial section on religion. The editor of *This Week* Sunday supplement magazine should also get a letter from you about his religious editorials and articles. Do the same when "big" magazines such as *The Saturday Evening Post* publish religious material. Let's not sit on our hands when some editor deserves applause. Your letters-to-the-editor can be a major factor in influencing his policies.

Naturally the same written encouragement should be sent to the radio and television stations which put on religious broadcasts. The more your local people see and hear religious news and religious articles, the more help you have in building up your congregation. For these are all reminders of Christ's way of life and build up the desire to come closer to "His way" through church attendance and through worship.

Another function of the publicity committee would be to arrange for the writing, designing, and placement of advertisements, or paid announcements.

The Episcopal Churches in Buffalo got together and put on a co-operative paid newspaper advertising campaign. The main illustration and copy sold the idea of attending church. Then each church had a listing of its name, minister, and location. The leading local advertising agency prepared the advertising campaign without any charge for its services. At the suggestion of the agency executive handling the campaign, the messages appeared on well-read local news pages, instead of the church page. This strategy assured the attention and readership of people who do not ordinarily read the church news on the Saturday or Sunday church page.

The art work for the Buffalo Co-operative Advertisements was supplied by the National Headquarters of the Episcopal Church. The headquarters of other denominations also offer excellent material for the preparation of newspaper advertising.

Another source of attractive illustrations and interesting, convincing messages are the effective newspaper advertisements prepared by the Home-Church-School Foundation.

This nonsectarian, nonprofit organization was established and is led by Mr. Cliff Scott of Little Rock, Arkansas. Mr. Scott's basic philosophy in this Foundation work is as follows:

> "Home–Church–School. These are the three institutions which contribute most to the moral and spiritual health and intellectual integrity of this nation."

Do You Remember That Christmas?

THE vision of Christmas to most of us is the Christmas of our childhood. The sweeping branches of a great evergreen sparkling and gay with ornament and ropes of tinsel. The exciting and colorful gifts grouped around its base. The huge table groaning with goodies. The sound of tinkling sleigh bells in the crisp air. The squeak of snow under our feet as the family trudged off to Service. The angelic beauty of the choir (miraculously transformed from the friends and neighbors we knew so well). The soul-stirring refrain of the lovliest songs the world has ever known . . . the carols. The feeling of deep peace and contentment as we too helped celebrate our most-honored Birthday.

It's a Christmas you'd like to live over again, wouldn't you? And you can even in these war-torn days with so many loved faces absent from the family get-together. Let your church help. If you are not a regular church-goer you may be sure of a warm and sincere welcome at the Episcopal Church near your home. But where you go is not important. The important thing is that you do go. Important to you if you, too, remember that Christmas.

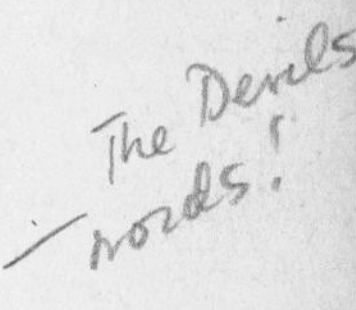

— THERE'S AN EPISCOPAL CHURCH NEAR YOUR HOME

ALL SAINTS' CHURCH, Linwood Ave. and West Ferry St. Rev. Sigfrid W. Sundin, Priest-in-Charge. Sunday Services: 8, 9:30 and 11 A. M.

CHURCH OF THE ASCENSION, North St. and Linwood Ave. Rev. Charles D. Broughton, D.D., Rector. Sunday Services: 8, 9:30 and 11 A. M.

CALVARY CHURCH IN AMHERST,

CHURCH OF THE HOLY COMMUNION, 770 Humboldt Parkway. Rev. E. C. Rorke, Rector. Sunday Services: 8 and 11 A. M.

MISSION OF OUR SAVIOUR, Modern Ave., Lackawanna. Mr. James Morgan, Layreader. Sunday Service at 11 A. M.

ST. ANDREW'S CHURCH, Main St. at Highgate Ave. Rev. Gordon L. Graser, Rector. Sunday Masses: 8, 9:30 and 11 A. M.

ST. MARY'S-ON-THE-HILL, Niagara and Vermont Sts. Rev. J. Jay Post, Rector. Sunday Services: 8, 9:30 and 11 A. M.

ST. MATTHEW'S HURCH, Seneca and Wasson Sts. Rev. Richard B. Townsend, Rector. Sunday Services: 8, 9:30 and 10:45 A. M.

ST. PAUL'S CATHEDRAL, Downtown at Shelton Square. Very Rev. Edward R. Welles, Dean. Sunday Services: 8, 9:30 and 11 A. M.

'ST. SIMON'S CHURCH, 200 Cazenovia St. Rev. Frank Blackwelder, Rector. Sunday Services: 8:30 and 11 A. M.

ST. STEPHEN'S CHURCH, Bailey Ave. at Hazel Pl. Rev. Howard W. Wilson, Rector. Sunday Services: 8 and 11 A. M.

ST. THOMAS' CHURCH, 501 South

The twenty-one newspaper advertisements prepared by the Home-Church-School Foundation are also a fine source of material for your church bulletins. Write for a free copy today. The address of the Home-Church-School Foundation is National Press Building, Washington 4, D.C., or write direct to Mr. Cliff Scott, Little Rock, Arkansas.

One of the best and the surest ways to publicize your church is to use small space announcements in Saturday local newspapers. Successful businesses have found that newspapers reach people effectively at a low cost. In your newspaper advertisements or announcements be sure to include the title of the sermon. This is essential even if the minister has to announce a change in the title at the service. The last line in your announcement should invite the reader to come to your church. This can be done with lines such as these:

WORSHIP WITH US SUNDAY
WORSHIP WITH US
FREE PEWS—VISITORS WELCOME

The First Baptist Church of White Plains, New York, found a way to increase attendance through the consistent use of small weekly newspaper ads. These were prepared by Allen B. Sikes, a member of this growing congregation. He developed a series of two-column by two-inch ads. Each had an attention-getting headline—an urge to go to church (any church)—an invitation to listen to the radio broadcast of the First Baptist's Sunday service, the subject of the sermon, and a picture of the minister. (See page 89 for examples of these advertisements.)

Mr. Sikes says these weekly ads have considerable favorable comment, and have been a major factor in increasing Sunday attendance.

Imagine the effect of this full-page newspaper ad on your members, neighbors and prospective members. A series of these messages are available in mat form by writing the Foundation at 516 Southern Building, Washington, D.C. Get your local newspaper and/or local merchants to sponsor this campaign. It will drive home the fundamental truths that we should all live by. →

"WHERE ARE MY WANDERING PARENTS TONIGHT?"

"Every night my mother used to tell me stories and say prayers with me before I went to sleep. Then she and Daddy got mad at each other. And he went off and she had to get a job and leave me at a boarding house. No one ever hears my prayers now. I wonder where my mother and daddy are tonight? And what will become of me?"

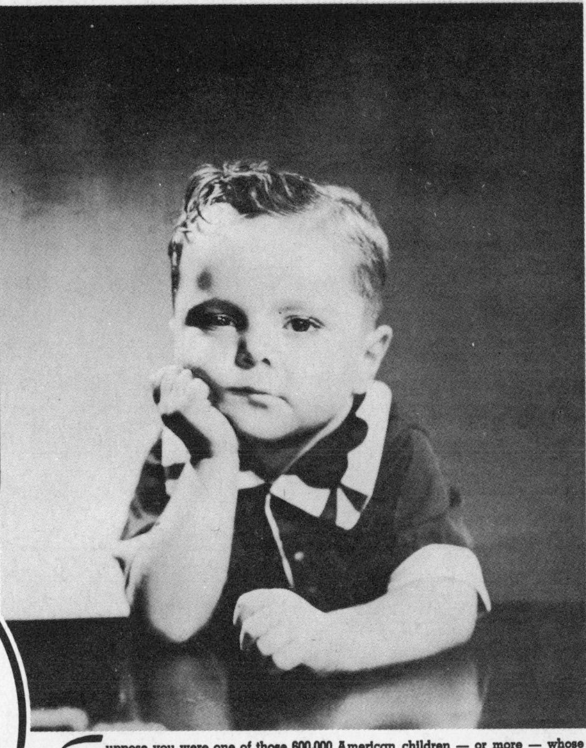

We wonder, too!

Suppose you were one of those 600,000 American children — or more — whose homes will be broken by divorce this year?

Suppose your parents were so careless, so thoughtless or indifferent that they wandered off in search of selfish pleasure and left you to grow up just any old way?

... WOULD YOU THINK IT FAIR?

This year at least 300,000 homes will be wrecked and more than twice that number of children will suffer because parents have failed in their greatest responsibility.

There was a time when divorce was considered such a disgrace that men and women would make any sacrifice to avoid it. Now it is becoming such an accepted thing that it is a national menace.

Too often the cause is "liquor or lipstick" according to the authorities. Drinking and casual affairs that may have started as thoughtless flirtations can result in domestic tragedy.

"Divorce actions . . . charging cruelty due to intoxicating liquor . . . greatly increased in 1944 . . . I have been amazed at the number of instances where I had to deprive mothers of the care of their children because of their inordinate use of . . . liquor". . . .

Judge William R. McKay,
Los Angeles Supreme Court

The
HOME - CHURCH - SCHOOL *Foundation, Inc.*

EDUCATIONAL ∾ Non-Legislative ∾ Non-Sectarian ∾ Non-Profit

WASHINGTON, D. C.

Join our national educational campaign to maintain and extend the influence of HOME-CHURCH SCHOOL for individual happiness and national survival. Your $5-$10-$25-$50-$100 annual membership in this foundation will give you a share in this all important work.

SERVING THE COMMUNITY

CHARLES O. WRIGHT, D.D.

MILLIONS OF AMERICANS

Will be in church Sunday morning to worship God—to thank Him for His countless blessings. Will you be among them?
For those unable to go—the First Baptist Church of White Plains broadcasts its Sunday morning service, WFAS (123) between 11 and 12.

Sermon topic

"How To Have Confidence In Yourself"

"Elijah" — Nov. 21 — 4 P.M.

Corner Maple & Mamaroneck Aves.

CHARLES O. WRIGHT, D.D.

ONLY 2 SUNDAYS LEFT BEFORE CHRISTMAS

Two opportunities to join with your family and neighbors in your church's vital Sunday morning service.

In case you cannot go—worship by radio with the First Baptist Church of White Plains, WFAS (123) between 11-12 A.M.

SERMON TOPIC

"HOW TO JOURNEY WITH JOY"

Corner Mamaroneck and Maple Avenues

"MESSIAH"—Sunday, Dec. 26—4 P.M.

CHARLES O. WRIGHT, D.D.

A FAMILY AFFAIR

Going to Church together AS A FAMILY is a thrilling experience. Plan on going Sunday to your Church.

If you cannot—listen to First Baptist Church service broadcast WFAS (123) Sunday morning 11-12.

Sermon topic

"How To Make Your Life Count"

Corner Maple & Mamaroneck Aves.

CHARLES O. WRIGHT, D.D.

AS AN AMERICAN

You have the right to go to the church you prefer. If you are unable to go next Sunday, worship by radio with the First Baptist Church, WFAS (123) between 11 and 12 Sunday morning.

Sermon topic

"What Is There In It For Me?"

(A complete service)

Corner Maple & Mamaroneck Aves.

CHARLES O. WRIGHT, D.D.

THE CRUX OF THE MATTER

Countless men and women right here in White Plains will better face the responsibilities of the week BECAUSE they spend part of Sunday morning worshipping God in the church of their choice. Will you be among them?

Those unable to attend are invited to worship by radio with the First Baptist Church, WFAS (123) 11-12. Sermon topic

"How To Be Happy Every Day"

Corner Maple & Mamaroneck Aves.

CHARLES O. WRIGHT, D.D.

GIVING **THANKSGIVING** THANKS

Sunday morning in your church will be a time when you can give thanks for the many blessings you and yours have received—make sure to be there.
If you are unable to—worship by radio with First Baptist Church, WFAS (123) 11-12 Sunday morning

Sermon topic

"How To Put Life Into Thanksgiving"

Corner Mamaroneck and Maple Avenues

Sunday—Elijah—4 P. M.

CHARLES O. WRIGHT, D.D.

HOME FOR THANKSGIVING

You'll always remember the hour you and your whole family spend in your church on Sunday morning.

If you are unable to attend the First Baptist Church of White Plains broadcasts its morning service on WFAS (123) between 11 and 12. Won't you listen?

Sermon Topic

"EVEN YOU CAN HELP GOD"

Corner Mamaroneck and Maple Avenues

CHARLES O. WRIGHT, D.D.

"AND THE WEAK SHALL BE MADE STRONG"

In other days—other troubled, uncertain times—men have found the clear straight road through Christianity. Be in your church Sunday morning to worship, to hear again the ageless promise of life.
If you are unable to go—worship by radid with First Baptist Church, WFAS (123) 11-12 Sunday morning.

Sermon Topic

"Something To Boast About"

Corner Maple and Mamaroneck Aves.

MORE THAN 250,000 COPIES OF ADS IN THIS SERIES HAVE APPEARED IN THE WHITE PLAINS REPORTER-DISPATCH.

I'm Serious!
Maybe you like smiling babies? Sorry to disappoint you, but I've got a lot on my mind.
There's something wrong in America . . . and I'm the chap who is getting hurt!
Our Constitution says that no one can be denied the right to worship God. I'm an American! According to the Constitution I have the right to learn about God, to hear the Bible Stories, to be taught the Christian Way of Life.
But here's the hitch. While the Government can't deny me the right to attend Church School and Church—MY PARENTS CAN. They can rob me of my most sacred right just by neglecting my spiritual needs.
Did you know that about half the children in America are growing up without religious training? And yet there's a church in every village!
Yessir, I'm serious! Instead of *talking* about juvenile delinquency, we ought to *do something* about it. We ought to crowd our churches with children . . . and parents! And we ought to start Sunday!
HOLY BIBLE
THE CHURCH FOR ALL . . . ALL FOR THE CHURCH
The Church is the greatest factor on earth for the building of character and good citizenship. It is a storehouse of spiritual values. Without a strong Church, neither democracy nor civilization can survive. There are four sound reasons why every person should attend services regularly and support the Church. They are: (1) For his own sake. (2) For his children's sake. (3) For the sake of his community and nation. (4) For the sake of the Church itself, which needs his moral and material support. Plan to go to church regularly and read your Bible daily.
Book Chapter Verses
Sunday . . . . . Mark 4 26-32
Monday . . . . . Matthew 25 1-13
Tuesday . . . . . John 6 1-14
Wednesday . . . . . Ephesians 6 1-4
Thursday . . . . . Proverbs 22 1-6
Friday . . . . . Psalms 103 13-18
Saturday . . . . . Matthew 18 1-6
Copyright 1949, E. E. Keister, Strasburg, Va.

This is another example of the fact that a church does not need to spend a lot of money publicizing its services. It's the consistency and continuity which count.

E. E. Keister, of Strasburg, Virginia, has developed a most effective program for presenting the Church's story to the unchurched. Drawing on his thirty years' experience as a successful publisher, he has prepared a series of attractive yet dignified newspaper advertisements aimed primarily at the nonchurchgoer. These powerful messages are designed for co-operative use by church and civic forces of a community in the secular press. Two examples are shown in this manual.

Mr. Keister believes that most of the church advertising in newspapers is of interest only to the "faithful few." Therefore his messages are directed at the great body of outsiders; the approach of each piece of copy is affirmative rather than negative. Co-operating in the preparation of the messages are newspaper editors, ministers, and laymen. Though Mr. Keister's messages are a recent development, they are already appearing in over 200 newspapers. In some cities such as Lexington, Kentucky; Montreal, Canada; Albert Lea, Minnesota; and Huntsville, Alabama, the newspaper space is paid for by a single sponsor. These commercial sponsors are business concerns of high moral standing in the community.

In other cities the "Support The Church" newspaper messages have a group sponsorship. In Toledo, Ohio, it's the Lutheran Churches —in Logansport, Indiana, the Logansport Ministerial Association— and in Ludington, Michigan, the Mason County Ministerial Association. Group sponsorship reduces the cost per advertisement for each sponsor to a small amount.

Read the above copy and you'll see why these Keister church ads are now appearing regularly in almost 500 newspapers, located in more than 30 states and three Canadian provinces. These newspaper ads are available in 5-column and 3-column widths. They can be sponsored by local merchants, or by churches, or run alone by the paper on its church page. ←

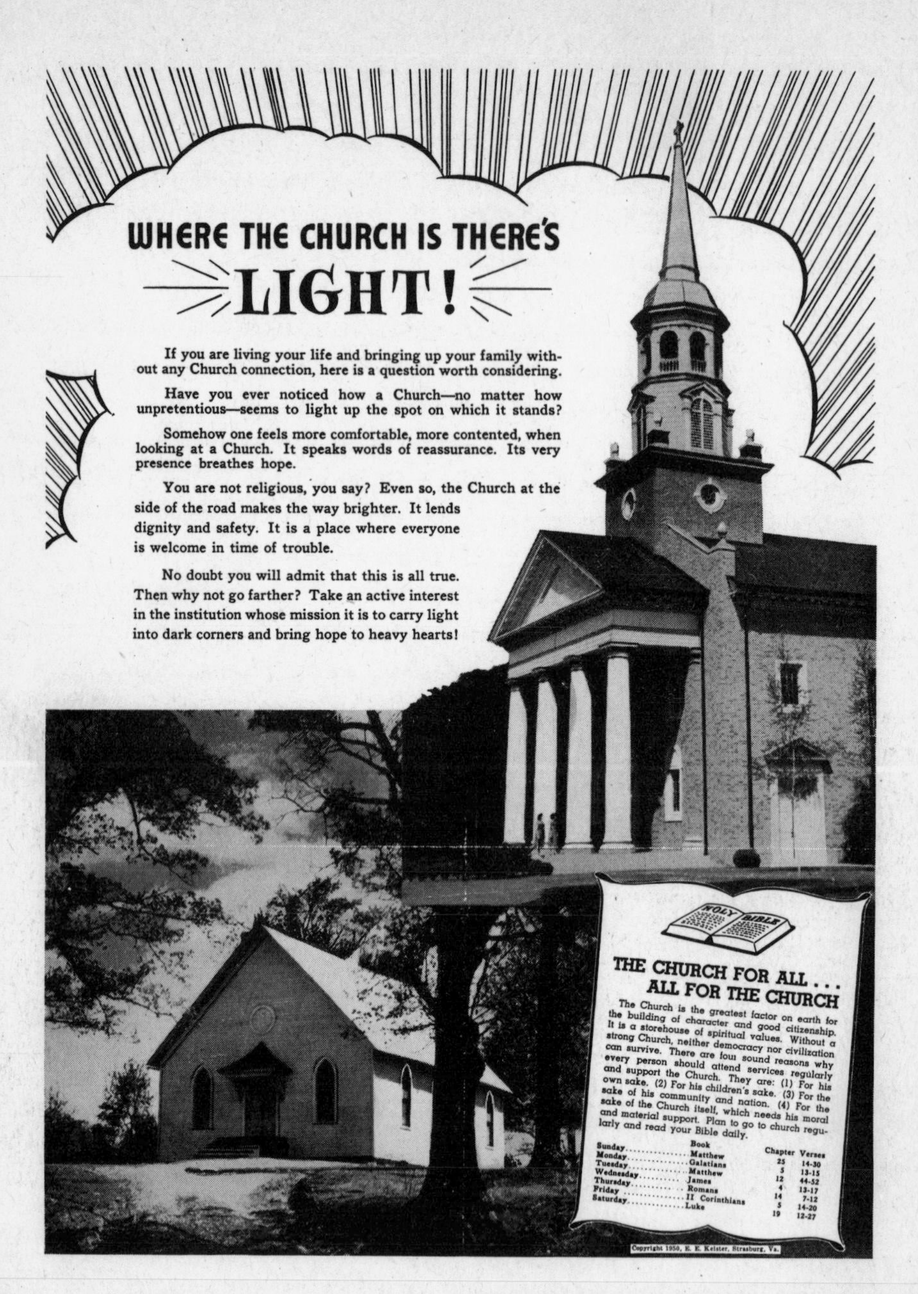

WHERE THE CHURCH IS THERE'S
LIGHT!
If you are living your life and bringing up your family without any Church connection, here is a question worth considering.
Have you ever noticed how a Church—no matter how unpretentious—seems to light up the spot on which it stands?
Somehow one feels more comfortable, more contented, when looking at a Church. It speaks words of reassurance. Its very presence breathes hope.
You are not religious, you say? Even so, the Church at the side of the road makes the way brighter. It lends dignity and safety. It is a place where everyone is welcome in time of trouble.
No doubt you will admit that this is all true. Then why not go farther? Take an active interest in the institution whose mission it is to carry light into dark corners and bring hope to heavy hearts!
HOLY BIBLE
THE CHURCH FOR ALL . . .
ALL FOR THE CHURCH
The Church is the greatest factor on earth for the building of character and good citizenship. It is a storehouse of spiritual values. Without a strong Church, neither democracy nor civilization can survive. There are four sound reasons why every person should attend services regularly and support the Church. They are: (1) For his own sake. (2) For his children's sake. (3) For the sake of his community and nation. (4) For the sake of the Church itself, which needs his moral and material support. Plan to go to church regularly and read your Bible daily.
Book Chapter Verses
Sunday..............Matthew 25 14-30
Monday..............Galatians 5 13-15
Tuesday..............Matthew 12 44-52
Wednesday..........James 4 13-17
Thursday............Romans 14 7-12
Friday..............II Corinthians 5 14-20
Saturday............Luke 19 12-27
Copyright 1950, E. E. Keister, Strasburg, Va.

Over 275 different advertisements have been prepared by Keister Advertising Service. Each message pays off with the basic theme, "The Church for All . . . All for the Church," and gives four sound reasons for attending church. The Bible readings are constructive suggestions.

The mats for producing the advertisements in the newspaper are in three widths: five-column, six-column, and seven-or-eight-column (for full pages). The height of the different sizes is in proper proportion. Mats can be obtained by writing directly to E. E. Keister, c/o Keister Advertising Service, Strasburg, Virginia. Any church or group contemplating a citywide cultivation of nonchurchgoers would do well to write Mr. Keister for his plan and copies of the letters he has received on its effectiveness.

Another source of fine support to religious thinking and religious giving is the new campaign developed by The Advertising Council. This organization represents leading advertising agencies and advertisers. Its members contribute their time and talents in developing advertising campaigns which promote worth-while causes. On pages 94 and 95 are examples of their excellent advertisements.

This is the challenging poster which was developed by the Advertising Council and United Church Canvass. 5,000 of them have been displayed at no charge for the benefit of religion by the Outdoor Advertising Industry, 60 East 42nd Street, New York, N.Y. Write any of these three sources for full information.

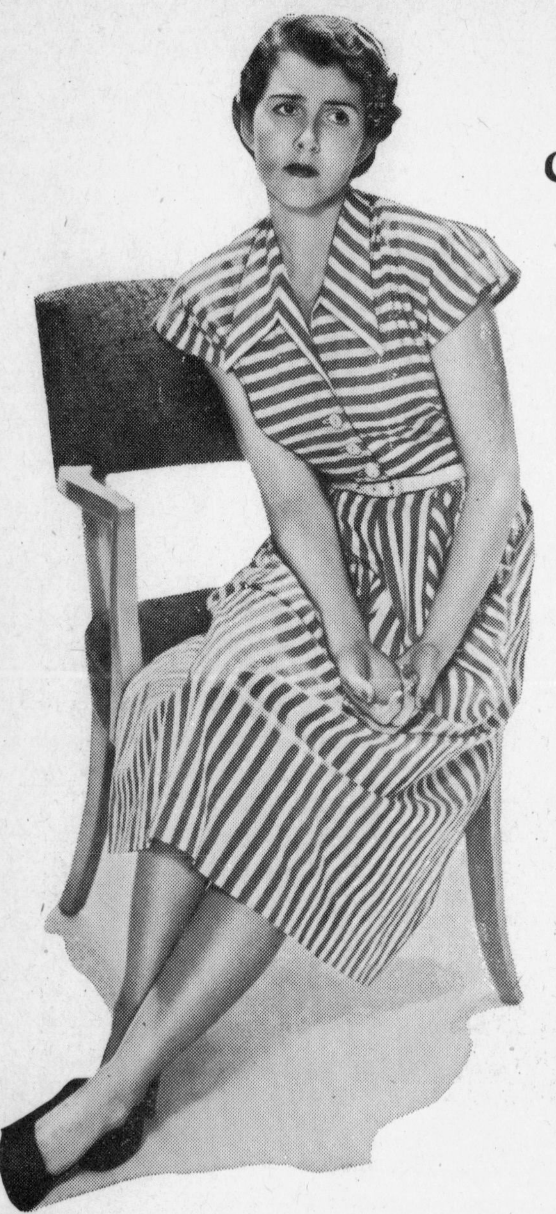

Has trouble come into your home?

If things are somehow taking a turn for the worse . . . if worry and unhappiness have replaced the peace of mind you used to know . . . think of this: Maybe what makes it seem so hard to handle is not the trouble itself, but *the way you face up to it!*

For whittling a worry down to size calls for a certain kind of strength, a certain point of view. The kind you get from church.

Nothing can take the place of church in your life—in anyone's life.

By turning to religion, by reaffirming their faith, new thousands every day are gathering new strength, new hope, new courage.

Families, finding themselves through faith, are being brought closer . . . becoming *real* families, strong against the world, happier, more tolerant among themselves.

Young folk, finding themselves through faith, are learning the true values that make them want to spurn the false.

Men and women of the workaday world are gaining a new sense of "the balance of things" . . . the *inner* security that brings success to work as well as to life . . . by finding themselves through faith.

Can you honestly say that things have been better for *you*, going it alone? Or wouldn't you rather join these neighbors . . . and find a happier, more successful life—through faith!

Mary Margaret McBride: "I want to make a plea for neglected children. I mean the boys and girls growing up without religious teaching, without knowing that happiness and goodness are related. They will thank you always for taking them to church now."

Find yourself through <u>faith</u>—**come to church this week**

Worried over your future?

"Is there anyone who isn't?" Before you say that . . . look around you. At certain folks you know in your community. At famous ones you read about as well. The ones who seem to have a kind of strength, an inner confidence, a point of view that makes them seem *so sure* of where they're going. It can't be just coincidence that these are the men and women who—*go to church!*

For nothing can take the place of church in your life—in anyone's life.

By turning to religion, by reaffirming their faith, new thousands every day are gathering new strength, new hope, new courage.

Families, finding themselves through faith, are being brought closer...becoming real families, strong against the world, happier, more tolerant among themselves.

Young folk, finding themselves through faith, are learning the true values that make them want to spurn the false.

Men and women of the workaday world are gaining a new sense of "the balance of things" . . . the *inner* security that brings success to work as well as to life . . . by finding themselves through faith.

Can you honestly say that things have been better for *you*, going it alone? Or wouldn't you rather join these neighbors . . . and find a happier, more successful life—through faith!

Roger W. Straus: "Whenever I feel tired or discouraged it is my custom to turn my thoughts to God, if possible in a synagogue; if not, wherever I may be. Never yet have I done so without being refreshed and encouraged."

Find yourself through faith —come to church this week

PHOTO: JAMES VILES

Contributed in behalf of the Religion In American Life Campaign by

(NAME OF SPONSOR)

The campaign on and for religion is called "Religion in American Life." It is sponsored by the Federal Council of Churches of Christ in America, the National Synagogue Council of America, and eighteen other religious bodies. The volunteer advertising agency which created the campaign was J. Walter Thompson of New York City. Proofs of the advertisements can be obtained by writing to the Advertising Council, Inc., 25 West 45th Street, New York City. These advertisements will give you some excellent ideas for your own church promotional material.

16

The United Church Canvass

THIS is one of the most successful ways for churches and synagogues to conduct their publicity campaign. The United Church Canvass warrants the serious consideration of your church and all the churches in your community.

In brief, the idea back of this tried and tested program is this: Churches and synagogues of a local community hold simultaneously, during a specified period of time, their member enlistment and financial campaigns. Each church conducts its own individual campaign as usual. However, it unites with a community committee which presents over the radio and through the newspapers, and other channels of publicity, a general appeal for the total religious program of the community.

Churches which, for various reasons, cannot co-operate in the financial phases of the canvass often join it in the use of promotional literature, stewardship materials, and world relief emphases. The by-products obtained are valuable.

One layman, one pastor, or one executive secretary is sufficient to start the plan in a local area. Once it is begun, the United Church Canvass wins many enthusiastic supporters for IT WORKS and produces "profits," both spiritually and financially.

All United Church Canvass Posters are reproductions from original paintings. Lithographed in four full colors, they are appealing and worshipful. Liberal space is provided at the bottom of each poster for your own imprint or worship theme.

For a decade or more, a few communities have been experimenting with a simultaneous approach to the people for financial support of their religious institutions. Churches and synagogues of a local area began to conduct their financial campaigns during the same period of time. Wartime pressures prompted interest and inquiries from other communities which led a group of national executives to form an interdenominational committee to help with publicity, literature, and counsel.

The United Church Canvass movement has grown, from a handful of communities in 1941, to over 350 in 1950. It has spread to every state in the union, to Canada, Gatun in the Canal Zone, and to Honolulu, Hawaii. It is coming to be known as a most effective way to promote the general work of all the churches and synagogues—simultaneously—and to raise maximum, rather than minimum, budgets for the ensuing year. This community operation is sponsored, supported, and promoted by nineteen major national religious denominations and bodies. These include the Federal Council of Churches of Christ in America, Church World Service, and the National Synagogue Council of America.

The advantages and goals of the United Church Canvass movement include the following:

1. To bring forcefully to the attention of the entire community the importance and necessity of our local religious institutions.
2. Cultivating the loyalty of the constituency in all religious bodies.
3. Developing systematic and proportionate giving habits among the adherents of the interfaith institutions.
4. Spiritualizing the financial resources of the community in support of these vital organizations.
5. Two periods of simultaneous cultivation. Communions whose fiscal year is synchronized with the calendar year have found the fall period more satisfactory. Those following a different fiscal year have found the spring period more suitable. Each community can determine the time most acceptable.

Must she Worship...Alone?

This is typical of the attractive, colorful posters which can be secured from the headquarters office of United Church Canvass. Other material features the slogan or theme of the 1949 campaign, "When the Church Bell Rings . . . say YES."

6. The advantage of national publicity through magazine, press, and radio on the essential ministry of religious institutions to the community, the nation, and the world.
7. The services of a national office in New York City are available to co-operate with denominational agencies and local councils of churches in promoting the canvass program.
8. Churches using this plan can secure a wealth of material for use of committees and workers. Best of all, this expertly created and proven material is available at much lower cost than it had been when produced locally and individually for co-operating churches. This campaign material includes the following: Work Kit Binder, Handbook for Action, Posters, Newspaper Mats, Broadsides, Audio-visual Aids, Film Strips, Recorded and Live Radio Spot Announcements, Folders, Publicity Suggestions, Training Booklets for Canvassers, Suggested Copy for Solicitation Letters, and Church Bulletins.

Two typical examples of results are:

a. Successful canvassers in New Haven obtained increases in pledges amounting to 10%, 15%, 41%, 57%, 85%.
b. Thirty-nine churches and synagogues in Greater Portland, Maine, averaged $23.42 in United Church Canvass expense, obtained $700,000 in pledges.

For complete details, get in touch with the Reverend Earle B. Pleasant, Executive Secretary of the United Church Canvass, Churchworld Building, 214 East 21st Street, New York 19, New York. The Reverend Mr. Pleasant will be glad to send you samples of the material which is available and answer your questions. Even if you cannot get a United Church Canvass started for this year, you may want to use some of the outstanding campaign material for your own church campaign.It can be adapted to your requirements with real effectiveness.

17

Don't Forget Direct Mail

WHEN we were discussing fund-raising we noticed the effectiveness of letters, booklets, and reply cards. Successful companies have also proved that direct mail methods can get people to do things at a low cost-per-response. Some firms conduct their entire sales campaign through the mail. Many charities obtain most of their support through mail solicitations.

Despite all this proof, too many churches neglect direct mail in canvassing members for annual pledges or raising money for special funds. Some are under the false impression that direct mail is too expensive. That is only so when the appeal is not properly presented. A local sales or advertising man can help a church present its appeal in an effective way. A local letter shop can do the same thing. The national headquarters of the various denominations can be of assistance and in many cases have fund-raising material which can be obtained at a fraction of its normal local cost.

Remember, it takes a little money to raise money. So don't look just at the initial cost of direct mail. Figure the cost on three bases:

1. How many pennies it takes to reach a prospect.
2. The time saved for canvassers in preparing the recipient to subscribe quickly and more generously.
3. The time saved in not having to call on those who mail in their subscription cards.

Judge your costs in relation to the total amount of money to be raised and the number of prospects to be solicited. Then you will agree with many successful companies that direct mail is a low-cost way of reaching and influencing people.

There is another valuable use of direct mail which is employed by successful stores, insurance companies, and other successful businesses. I refer to the "Letter of Welcome" sent to people and families who have just moved into a city, community, or neighborhood. This letter welcomes the newcomers and offers to be of service. Here is how it can, and *is* used by progressive churches.

> Dear Mr. and Mrs. (name of newcomers)
>
> We are pleased to welcome you to (name of city, community, or neighborhood). It is a friendly place and we do hope you and your family will like it here.
>
> If we can be of any assistance in giving you information on the facilities in your new neighborhood, don't hesitate to phone (number) or drop us a note. It would be a privilege for us to be of help to you.
>
> Should you not find a church of your denomination in this section of the city, we would like to have you worship with us at (name of church). Our Sunday service begins at (time). Your chilwhen would be more than welcome at our Sunday school. If you did not have a church home in your former location, do let (name of church) be your neighborhood friend in (name of place).
>
> (hand-signed by minister)

Notice how the last paragraph prevents you from being criticized for proselytizing. For your invitation is only directed at those who have no church connections in your neighborhood.

The names of newcomers are found in the newspapers. Also ask your regular members to send you the names of new families moving into their neighborhoods. To follow up the letter, you can appoint a chairman of a "Welcoming Committee" to call on the new people.

18

The Church Newsletter

FOR full effectiveness from weekly bulletins, large churches should mail copies to their active membership. The infrequent attender is thus regularly informed of the church life, its various activities, and services. A digest of the past week's sermon is a helpful subject for this mailing.

However, many churches do not mail these newsletters because they are afraid of the cost. They do not realize that it can be cut to only one cent per bulletin by using the bulk-mailing rate. You will have to make an application at your local post office. There will be a $10 fee payable each January first to enable you to continue mailing bulletins at this rate. There is also a $10 fee for a permit to mail matter without a stamp affixed. This permit remains in force as long as your church makes one mailing every twelve months.

Alternatively, you can get the bulletin entered as second-class matter for from $25 up (for mailings of 2,000 or less pieces) which cuts postage to only one cent per pound. Your bulletin must be published weekly (you can suspend publication during the summer); one half of the editorial content must be of general interest; and you must supply the local post office with a bona fide subscription list. This list is made by adding to your pledge card: "Seventy-five cents is for my subscription to the (name of bulletin) for the current year." Then your pledge list is your subscription list. Consult your local post office about the details of these arrangements.

Some churches use the back cover of their bulletin to list the heads of their various organizations. This list of leading church workers and the organizations is helpful and impressive. It is a cross section of fine people who support and work for the church. This influences visitors and non-members.

People who do attend church like to know the books which are recommended by the minister. The church newsletter is an excellent place to list the recommended titles.

When the attendance at your church is showing an increase, put that good news in the church bulletin. Compliment the congregation for its interest and faithfulness. Inspire the members to continue making new records for attendance.

If your church prints its weekly newsletter, why not have each Communion Sunday issue printed in purple. Purple is the church's own color. It signifies church and religion more than any other color. Therefore, purple is an effective color to use for printed material, outside signs, and bulletin boards.

The churches which put out weekly bulletins for services should take advantage of swapping ideas with each other. The editor of each bulletin should exchange weekly copies with six to ten other churches whose bulletins he admires.

The editor of the weekly bulletin would find it helpful to build a file of inspirational statements made by well-known people. These make excellent additions to the bulletin. Here are a few examples:

General Dwight Eisenhower: "What we need today is a dynamic constructive force to lead the world . . . except for moral regeneration, there is no hope for us, and we are going to disappear one day in the dust of an atomic explosion."

Mary Margaret McBride: "I want to make a plea for neglected children. I mean the boys and girls growing up without religious teaching, without knowing that happiness and goodness are related. They will thank you always for taking them to church now."

Dale Carnegie: "I spent several years writing a book on How to Stop Worrying and Start Living. After years of research, I am convinced that the best possible method for conquering worry is prayer and religious faith."

Sister Elizabeth Kenny: "What success I have had in helping others would have been quite impossible without a boundless faith in the ability of the spirit to triumph over the flesh."

J. H. Doolittle: "Religion, to me, is recognition of God and the conduct of life in accordance with his precepts. It requires adherence to the Golden Rule and eschews the law of expediency (that the end justifies the means). It is exemplified in the worship of God, in kindness, unselfishness, honesty, decency, morality and purity."

19

Making Use of Radio and Television

MANY churches find that the broadcasting of their Sunday services is a positive help in building up their congregations. The unusual popularity of religious programs such as "The Greatest Story Ever Told" is additional evidence that radio listeners want religious broadcasts. They find them a big help in trying to lead a Christlike life. Therefore churches should do everything possible to use the tremendous influence of radio in reaching prospective churchgoers and church members.

If it is not possible to broadcast the services, your church could probably persuade a local radio station to use the recorded meditations supplied by "The Upper Room" of Nashville, Tennessee. The title of these fifteen-minute devotionals is "Families Who Pray Together, Stay Together." Another excellent source is the George Logan Price organization at 946 South Normandie Avenue, Los Angeles (6), California. For fifteen years George Logan Price has been directing the production and distribution of transcribed Bible drama. He can give you the success stories of local companies that have sponsored religious broadcasts and built public good will, good will that more than paid for the costs of the programs.

See if some member of your church, who uses local advertising for his business, will sponsor the broadcasting of recorded religious programs. Fan mail and surveys prove that businesses sponsoring such programs build up unusual good will for their company and products. In addition, the popularity of the program enables the advertiser to reach the best type of family at a very low cost.

So many people turn to radio for information and entertainment, that it is a fine place to transmit the great truths of the Bible to churchgoers and prospective members.

More and more churches are getting the opportunity to reach local families through local television stations. Business has proved that this new medium for reaching people has the greatest impact, the deepest influence on reviewers. That is because television combines sight with sound.

If you have one or more television stations in your city, call on the station manager or program director. Tell him about your forthcoming special services, which warrant televising. If necessary, agree to pay for part of the cost of bringing television equipment to your church. Some prominent member of the congregation is usually willing to pay for such unusual church service, perhaps as a memorial to a loved one.

If it is not possible to telecast from your church, offer the services of your choir for a station studio broadcast. They could sing the music for a special Sunday service some time before or after the service on Sunday. These telecasts would help build up interest in attending your church and other local churches. Other churches would co-operate in offering the television station enough talent for a regular weekly program entitled "Choir of the Week."

All in all, television offers such vast promotional possibilities, it should not be ignored by churches as they seek to influence more and more people.

20

Other Promotional Plans That Work

IF you have a church bulletin board out in front of the church (and every church should have one), be sure it carries the following:

Title of Sermon	Name of Minister
Time of Service	Welcome to Visitors

1. During the week, the bulletin board should not be blank. It should show some inspirational thought. One of the best thoughts to show on the bulletin board repeatedly is the basic theme of your church publicity.
2. If your church can be reached easily from hotels, be sure a supply of your Sunday Service Bulletins is placed on the hotel reception desk Saturday night. Most hotel managers will co-operate in this respect. The Ralston Hotel in Columbus, Georgia, displays a framed invitation in the lobby, inviting the guests to worship at the First Baptist Church across the street.
3. A growing Eastern congregation arranges to pick up hotel guests and take them to and from the church. This helpful service is announced by a sign in the hotel lobby. The sign gives the time and place for meeting the friendly (free) transportation car.
4. Most people like to sign their names in public places. This is

especially true of visitors. So why not have a register book in your vestibule where the guests at the service can be recognized and a record made of their visit? It can be made more useful if once a year a letter is written to the visitors, inviting them to worship at the church whenever they are in town.

5. If I were a minister of a downtown church, or one that had a great number of visitors, I'd provide free picture post cards of the church and choir. Hotels, restaurants, railroads, and even radio people have found that the mailing of free post cards develops greater patronage from the recipients of the post card. Yes, I'd even pay for the postage stamps.

6. The Lutheran churches have done an outstanding job in using outdoor signs. These dignified, yet attractive, signs invite people to worship in their churches and direct visitors in a city to the Lutheran churches.

This shows how one Lutheran Church uses outdoor posters to increase both attendance at church, and listening over the air.

This big outdoor poster shows how the Lutheran Churches use the tested form of outdoor advertising to get people to listen to their radio program.

7. The stranger in a city, the visitor, the vacationist, the sightseer, are all ideal prospects for your Sunday service. If your church is located in a city where many visiting motorists spend week ends, you can use an outdoor invitation on main highways. A painted bulletin board just outside the city limits could carry an invitation something like this:

WORSHIP WITH US THIS SUNDAY
NAME OF CHURCH
TIME OF THE SERVICE
STREET LOCATION OF THE CHURCH

8. The flying of a church flag and the American flag over the outside church door can be arranged in most cases without taking the money from the regular budget. In nearly every church, there are several individuals or families who would like to give the flags as a memorial to some loved one.

The dedication of the flag or flags provides an opportunity to add additional interest to some Sunday service. Here is how the new church flag was described in the Bulletin of St. Bartholomew's Church in New York City.

"This morning we dedicate the new church flag, given by Mr. and Mrs. Harry M. Addinsell, to the Glory of God, and as a thank offering for His many blessings. This flag is the one flown over the door of the church.

"Our new church flag is a constant reminder to every passer-by of his duty and privilege as a child of God, to enter and share with a thankful heart in the worship of His Heavenly Father.

"To all of us in the fold, it should ever urge us to strengthen our own lives, and enthusiastically to do our utmost to carry the Good News of the Gospel of Jesus Christ to all men everywhere. The Church is the only organization in the world for proclaiming the Faith, and *we are the Church.*"

This is the prayer with which the congregation and clergy dedicated their new church flag:

"O Blessed Lord Jesus, we dedicate this flag to Thee as a symbol of Thy Church. Grant that wherever it is unfurled, it may be the emblem of liberty, justice, and truth. Grant that all who see it may be inspired to appreciate their privilege of membership in Thy Church and to realize that the protection it symbolizes brings to them the blessings of progress, education, and religion. May its white ever speak to us of purity: its red of that glowing zeal that pleaseth Thee: and its blue of the eternal home beyond the stars.

"May this flag ever stir humanity toward the attainment of a true brotherhood and hasten the time when, through the Church, the power of the Gospel shall bring all the nations to bow in adoration and loyalty before Thee, Who art both King of Kings and Lord of Lords, our only Lord and Saviour. Amen."

9. Like the flag, the church bell can be put to effective use. Why not ring the bell every noon, to indicate the midday and to remind all hearers of the church as their inspiration for Christ's way of life?

10. Many churches are located on main thoroughfares. This provides a constant flow of traffic, of people, of families. They should be reminded by night, as well as by day, that your church is there to help them, that all churches offer them something which cannot be obtained from any

other source. So check up and see if one or more of your stained-glass windows cannot be illuminated from within the church. Consider flood-lighting your steeple. Successful businesses have found that outside advertising reminds people to buy their products. Therefore, churches should use this same tested way to remind passers-by of their great service to all mankind.

11. Most churches have grounds which are large enough for a church garden. Why not use some of this space to have a showing of flowers, worthy of the Master, who loved flowers and referred to flowers in his talks? Some churches have room and will want to have their garden in form of a cross. Other churches may want their garden in one of the more usual designs. But either way, the garden should be in front of the church where all passers-by can enjoy it. A garden committee can handle this activity easily and with real pleasure for its members.

12. At Christmastime your church should show some special decoration, for the church is the original source of the Christmas celebration. At this time we honor Christ's birth. Therefore his organization on earth should show outward rejoicing. Some form of Christmas decoration should be used. If possible the Cradle Scene should be set up as a display in front of the Church to focus attention on the real meaning of Christmas. Let us not have stores and business show the Christmas spirit in decoration while the exterior of our churches carry no notice of this great religious season.

PLAN SHEET

Publicizing Your Church

1. *Publicity Committee*
   Chairman: ....
   Committee Members: ....
   ....
   ....
   ....

2. *Activities or Events to Be Publicized*
   ....
   ....

3. *Bulletin Board Committee*
   ....
   ....

4. *Contact with "Home-Church-School" Foundation*
   ....

5. *Committee for Roadside Bulletin*
   ....
   ....

6. *Chairman in Charge of Newspaper Announcements*
   ....

7. *Other Promotional Activities*
   ....
   ....

PART IV

A Word to the Wise

21

Additional Ideas and Suggestions

SOME wise man said, "Morale is a matter of little things." A recurring series of pleasant little things and events make most people feel better and brings them one form of happiness.

A successful business or a growing, influential church is also the result of having people pleased or satisfied with the way a lot of little things are done. That is why this book includes a chapter on "Additional Ideas and Suggestions." It discusses little things which, when well done, please more people and help build up a congregation.

1. Businessmen are accustomed to commercial speeches which end with specific suggestions of things to do, steps to take. They look for and respond to "closings" which outline a helpful or beneficial course of action or thinking. That is why businessmen often fail to get direct, personal good out of many sermons. They miss those final suggestions of what to do—how to carry out the basic idea of the sermon, how to lead a better, more helpful, more Christian life during the coming week. Many of the leading preachers always close their sermons with specific ideas of action. This what-to-do-about-it ending should be used in the close of most sermons.

2. Executives wonder why ministers do not take the same practical attitude about sermons which businessmen take about their talks. Some men can write a good speech or sales talk. But many men cannot. The successful executive who cannot write well gets some experienced

writer to write his speech, or he adapts a speech or article written by some outstanding speaker.

There are many ministers who find it difficult to write a good sermon. This is not their fault and is not held against them. However, they can help overcome this handicap by adapting the ideas of famous ministers to their individual congregations, cities, and local situations. Congregations would rather have an adapted version of a powerful, inspiring sermon (which they wouldn't hear otherwise) than a weak original by a minister who just can't write good sermons.

3. Serial stories in magazines and newspapers have proved that people like to have some thought continued, instead of completed, in one session. Too few ministers capitalize on the public's interest in serials by preaching sermons in series. This gives the unusual opportunity to urge attendance at subsequent services in order to get the complete thought and lesson of the sermon subject.

4. Many successful stores find that it is helpful to keep a rack of interesting booklets and folders just inside one of the entrances. An outstanding example of this practice is the R. H. Macy store in New York City.

What are the folders a church can distribute in this way? The available material includes the following:

Reprints of important sermons
History and organization of the church
Folders on foreign missions
Folders on special financial campaigns
Religious tracts
Copies of *The Upper Room*
Copies of religious magazines
Copies of *Guideposts*
Pocketbook on daily prayers

The Upper Room is the most widely used devotional guide. It is published bimonthly and contains daily devotions for family and individual use. *The Upper Room* is edited by J. Manning Potts, from their headquarters in Nashville, Tennessee. The cost is small enough to be within the means of every church. These daily devotionals are a sure way to keep members thinking about Christ and His Church all through the week. This helps to build up a congregation.

Guideposts magazine is composed of eloquent personal messages written by great leaders in our country. Edited by Norman Vincent Peale, it is a pocket-size magazine published monthly for a small charge. Managing Director of Guideposts Associates, Inc., is Frederic C. Decker, Pawling, New York. These spiritual publications are well worth sampling to your congregation.

5. When a member of the congregation is elected to a new office, gets a new and better job, or receives a fine promotion, a letter of congratulation from the minister is most welcome. This reminds the member that his church is interested in him personally, and of its desire to have him worship every Sunday. The information source of these letters is usually the news story in the local newspaper.

6. The Westwood Hills Church in Los Angeles pioneered in using a cartoon booklet which has been a big extra factor in increasing attendance and in paying off the mortgage. All this came about because Mark Hogue persuaded Jefferson Machamer to develop a booklet on going to church. This famous cartoonist produced one in his own unusual and popular style. The title is a startling one, *It's Fun to Go to Church*. After it was distributed house to house, attendance increased immediately. In fact, loud-speakers had to be installed in the church dining room, Sunday school rooms, vestry and wedding chapel. These are used to accommodate overflow crowds. Of course, what influences people in the suburbs of Los Angeles may not be of an equal influence in other communities. Yet the church worker who wants to get a new and different approach to building up attendance would do well to write the Westwood Hills Congregational Church, Los Angeles, for a copy of this booklet.

7. Some ministers find that they increase their male audience by offering prayers during the service for businessmen. They pray that both businessmen and employees will meet the problems of today in a Christian way. Some churches include prayers for businessmen in their weekly bulletins, so the male members can put them in their wallets for frequent use. Here is one from *The Upper Room*.

PRAYER FOR BUSINESS EXECUTIVES

Our heavenly Father, be with me through the coming business day. Help me to be Christian in all I do, say, and think. May I never take advantage of my position to hurt or hinder the welfare of my fellow workers. In all my relations with my associates and employees may I set an example of Christian living. In Christ's name. Amen.

8. When the churches in your city or your neighborhood are planning a co-operative effort, do not overlook the possibility of getting the support of the local posts of the American Legion. The Legionnaires are well known for their help in supporting and putting over worthwhile causes.

For example, Memphis Post No. 1 launched a campaign to "teach children religion." As the opening announcement, five hundred poster cards were placed in offices and churches. These featured the truism, "No Child Has a Chance Who Hasn't Been Taught to Pray and Love God." This campaign for youth was so successful that it was made a state-wide program.

Following up the fine example of Memphis, the American Legion Posts in Brooklyn, New York, organized a complete campaign built around the basic thought, "Teach Children Religion for a Better Community." A continuous schedule of posters sold this comparison: "Religion Means Reverence, Obedience, Order. Irreligion Means Chaos, Crime, Social Collapse. Parents Wake Up!" The first poster showed George Washington praying for divine guidance at Valley Forge. The "Four Chaplains," immortalized by their voluntary death on the S.S. Dorchester, illustrate the second poster.

Your community could be enriched spiritually by a similar campaign. Why not ask your ministers or council of churches to get together with the American Legion to discuss definite plans?

9. Most Christians and most churches, from time to time, carry out most of the activities which are part of Christ's Way of Life. Yet,

there is one major activity of a true Christian which is either neglected or completely ignored by most of us. That is found in Matthew 25:36: *"I was sick, and ye visited me: I was in prison and ye came unto me."*

How many of us have ever visited any of the unfortunates in prison? Who among us have sent encouragement to our brothers who are behind bars? Have any of us called recently on the local prison or jail to see what we could do personally to help rehabilitate the minds, attitudes, and the souls of prisoners? Remember that some of these prisoners of today will be rubbing elbows with us and our families tomorrow. For our own safety, if not for the greater unselfish motive, we should all assume the Christian responsibility of making sure that when the prisoners return to our outside world, they are ready to assume a self-respecting, self-supporting place in society. This objective can be achieved most completely when individuals take a personal interest in prisoners and augment the fine job being done by most penal institutions.

Right now you may be saying to yourself: "That's a worthy work. I'd like to be of help. But I've never called on prisoners. How do I start? What can I do? What do I do?" The answers to these vital questions can be secured from several sources. One is the Council of Churches in Louisville, Kentucky.

Individuals and churches who are interested in doing a real job in this greatly needed work, should write for a copy of the excellent booklet, "The Layman Helps the Warden," ably written by George Stoll, Chairman of the Council's Committee on Institutions. It is a documented case history of what two hundred men of Louisville are doing about prisons, jails, courts, hospitals, and child-care institutions. This booklet gives the complete details of the procedure which has made "The Louisville Plan" one of the greatest successes in this country. It explains exactly how other groups can duplicate and extend the fine work being done by the Louisville men.

Presidents of men's clubs, heads of church boards, officers of laymen's groups, and local councils of churches, or ministers, should write for a copy to: The Louisville Council of Churches, Louisville, Kentucky or to the publisher, Paul's Workshop, 241 East Walnut, Louisville 2 Kentucky. The small charge per copy covers only the cost of printing without any profit or royalty.

Individuals who wish to carry out a personal program of help to those in prison or institutions can get some excellent suggestions by writing to Lt. General John C. H. Lee, Executive Vice-President of the Brotherhood of St. Andrew, York, Pennsylvania. He has had considerable experience in helping to build back the morale and self-respect of prisoners. His training is also augmented by the activities of the Brotherhood of St. Andrew in establishing chapters in prisons.

10. The Fifth Avenue Presbyterian Church in New York City has developed a tested plan for building up corporate communion services which can be adapted by a church of any size in a city of any size. The plan is a simple yet very effective one. The congregation is divided up into districts, according to where the members live. Then layworkers visit the members in their district before the May and November communions.

The large Fifth Avenue Presbyterian parish is now divided into 111 districts in New York, New Jersey, and Connecticut. Covering this territory are 62 women, 38 men, and 13 married couples (working as a team). All these volunteers are earnest in their desire to develop a closer fellowship within the church membership. Their visitations start at least a month before the semiannual corporate Communion Sundays. The volunteer visitors are assigned to the districts in which they live. The latest report shows that their visits resulted in 1,347 parishioners receiving the blessed sacrament on one Sunday.

In addition to building up interest in special services, the visitors' calls uncover valuable information for the clergy and church offices. This covers cases of illness, special needs, changes of address, and availability of members' time for church work. Two special committees remain active the year round. One is for men and married couples, and the other for women.

The inspiration back of this successful plan is Dr. John Sutherland Bonnell, D.D., L.L.D., Minister of the Fifth Avenue Presbyterian Church. The best part of his visitation program is that it can be and is being adopted by churches of any and all sizes. For example, a congregation of 300 members is being divided into five geographical districts. The pastor plans to have a meeting with each district in its own neighborhood meetingplace at least once a year.

Another plan for building up the congregation developed by Dr. Bonnell is the formation of eight prayer groups. These groups are formed on the basis of age and interests. The length of their meetings varies from group to group depending largely on the type of program. Both of these plans do much in keeping members interested in and working for their church.

11. Have you ever heard of "The Christian Fuller Brush Man?" He is the Reverend Robert W. Anthony and he is as successful in selling the use of religious booklets as Fuller salesmen are in selling the use of their brushes. Here is how his plan works.

When he starts out to make parish calls, this pastor carries a regular business-executive's, or salesman's portfolio. One side is filled with samples of religious booklets, folders, leaflets, and cards to help parents in the Christian training of youth. In the other side of the case he carries an assortment of literature for adults: personal religion, inspiration for the perplexed aged, bereaved—and special prayers.

When there are children in the family, the Reverend Anthony shows the mother or father his assortment of booklets on youth training. Then he asks, "What is there here that you would like to have?" The member is usually interested in having one or two pieces. When a little child is present during the call, this pastor reads the child the story of "Why the Little Elephant Got Spanked" from a miniature-size book. Then he gives the child this attractively illustrated book—and he makes a warm friend for life.

On other calls, the Reverend Anthony shows and offers to adults literature of aid. On every call, he suggests and offers vision-uplifting material. He, like other ministers, has found that this literature is food. It nourishes the soul between church services and provides stimuli for daily meditations. Best of all, the Reverend Anthony has developed a practical way of using this literature to make every one of his parish calls more helpful and long remembered. The literature he carries into people's homes bears fruit in Christ-enriched lives.

Today is the ideal time for other ministers to adopt this tested method of building up their congregations. For the supply of well written, attractive booklets is greater than ever before. Every denominational house is ready to supply them. In addition, there are interdenominational agencies like: The Federal Council of Churches, The International Council of Religious Education, The Foreign Missions Conference, The American Tract Society, The Upper Room, and Guideposts.

Some businessman-member of your church would be glad to donate the brief case. And others can be asked to support the "Literature Fund" which makes possible this valuable distribution of helpful church literature.

12. This chapter on "Additional Ideas" closes with the following—one of the most important suggestions in the entire book. We might call it a "turnabout" or reciprocal suggestion.

The basic plan of this book is for clergymen and layworkers to use tested business methods in their high calling. Now we "turn about," and urge all businessmen to use religion in their business activities. Just as successful business methods can help build up a congregation, so can Christ's Way of Life build up a business on the right Christian basis.

You might ask, "How can I carry my religion into my business?" There are many ways—in addition to being a Christian in your daily relations to your employer, employees, and your customers. Here are just three examples:

a. The Nehi Corporation of Columbus, Georgia, opens each sales convention and company salesmen's meeting with a prayer. These prayers start the company's deliberations on a high plane of operations.

b. The Laymen's Committee for a Christian World, in New York City, has worked with labor leaders, management, and company personnel executives in getting union contract meetings opened with prayer. As Chairman Wallace C. Speers states it: "We earnestly urge you to seek through prayer the kind of guidance which will achieve mutually beneficial solutions, and give new vitality to the meaning of America as a God-given land where free men can elevate the common good above personal interest. Whatever the measure of your differences at the council table, however deep and sincere, we ask you constantly to bear in mind that as sons of God endowed with the priceless heritage of freedom, you have the opportunity to demonstrate again to the people of the earth that spiritually motivated men in our dynamic society can strive together with strength and humility for good of all."

c. General Robert Wood Johnson, Chairman of the Board of Directors of Johnson & Johnson, is well known for using Christian principles in his company's relationships with the public, employees, dealers, and stockholders. His "Code of Ethics" for all Johnson & Johnson companies is one of the finest business creeds in existence. Christian businessmen should write the J & J Company at New Brunswick, New Jersey, for a copy. It shows how Christianity can be a guide to successful business relations.

In a talk on "Welfare Capitalism," General Johnson uses this as an introductory explanation of the philosophy behind the Code:

"We should use as our guiding light in all matters the principles of Christianity. Let us look further into this last statement. A good start is the Sermon on the Mount. Here is the true policy of employment:

> 'Therefore all things whatsoever ye would that men should do to you, do ye even so to them; for this is the law and the prophets.' (Matthew 7:12)

"You may search all the thousands of books on management, and you will fail to find any policy as suitable.

"But this is a very general policy; to be effective, it must be interpreted in terms of the day-to-day events and problems of management. Here is our business code. It is our attempt to spell out the application of the Golden Rule."

This J & J code of ethics closes with: "We are determined, with the help of God's grace, to fulfill these obligations to the best of our ability."

This is an example of how hundreds of great and growing companies are building up their business on Christian principles. Therefore, the clergy and layworkers should urge businessmen and employees to take Our Lord's teachings into daily business, instead of considering His Way of Life as just an inspiration for Sundays.

22

Start Your Plans Today

THIS manual and the other books mentioned in previous chapters are filled with tested ideas for increasing your congregation. Yet, they are not self-starting. Someone has to put them into action. Make that someone you!

Remember the best way to start anything is to take the first step immediately, when you are thinking about it. So right now, before you put this book down:

1. Get a pencil or pen.
2. Decide which ideas you will start first.
3. Fill out the plan sheets on those ideas.

These handy plan sheets are an ideal first step. They provide a convenient place to:

1. Write in the data on your own church and congregation.
2. Jot down ways certain ideas which can be adapted to your church.
3. List names of potential workers and committee chairmen.
4. Put down dates when ideas can be carried out.

When you use the plan sheets in the above ways, you are starting to fill empty pews, the same tested way successful businessmen start their business-building activities.

The author sincerely hopes and prays that you have found this manual helpful and stimulating. However, his efforts in writing, and your time in reading this idea manual, are largely wasted unless you take the first step in using the plan sheets and following out the suggestions. Take that step right now! Your church has the greatest opportunity in history. Your friends and neighbors need Christ's teachings and way of life more than ever before. They are the only true and lasting guides to take us through these troublesome times.

PLAN SHEET

Other Promotional Plans That Work

1. Installation, and/or Greater Use of Outside Bulletin Board
....
....
....

2. & 3. Invitation Sign in Hotel Lobbies and Pickup for Guests
....
....
....

4. & 5. Guest Book for Vestibule and Free Post Cards
Chairman ....
....
....

6. Outside-of-City Bulletin for Visitors, Tourists
....
....
....

8. (Outside) Flying of Church Flag
....
....
....

9. Additional Ringing of Church Bell
....
....
....

10. Illumination of Spire and of Windows
Chairman ....
....
....

11. Arrangements for a Church Garden
Chairman ....
....
....

Additional Ideas and Suggestions

2. Books of Sermons
....
....
....

3. Subjects for Sermon Series
....
....
....

4. Literature Rack
Chairman ....
....
....

9. Calling on Prisons
Chairman ....
....
....

10. District Plan for Visiting
Chairman ....
....
....

11. Use-of-Literature Portfolio
....
....
....

Note: Numbers refer to numbered sections in Chapters 20 and 21.

23

List of Books on Publicity and Related Subjects

FOR BUILDING UP YOUR CONGREGATION

Courtesy of the Commission on Public Information of the Methodist Church, 150 Fifth Avenue, New York 11, N. Y., Ralph Stoody, Director

CHURCH PUBLICITY

General

HOW TO MAKE FRIENDS FOR YOUR CHURCH—By John L. Fortson. Association Press, N.Y.C. A manual by a former public relations director of the Federal Council of Churches.

PUBLIC RELATIONS FOR CHURCHES—By Stewart Harral. Abingdon-Cokesbury, N.Y.C., 1945, 135 pages. These "tested methods of winning goodwill for your church" include relation with the press, church printing and other advertising media, including direct mail.

SUCCESSFUL CHURCH PUBLICITY—By Carl F. H. Henry. Zondervan Publishing House, Grand Rapids, Mich., 1943. 246 pages. Traces history of religious journalism, and describes techniques.

Church and Press

CHURCH AND NEWSPAPER—By William B. Norton. The Macmillan Co., 1930. 260 pages. Not new, but an admirable treatise by the former religion editor of *Chicago Tribune*. Because the author was a minister the book is written with understanding both of church life and requirements of the newsroom.

KEEPING YOUR CHURCH IN THE NEWS—By W. Austin Brodie. Fleming H. Revell Co., N.Y.C., 125 pages. A handbook on methods of securing publicity through numerous media, written by a newspaper man.

Church Promotional Plans

CROWDED CHURCH A, Through Modern Methods. By Eugene Dinsmore Dolloff. Fleming H. Revell Co., N.Y., 1946. 147 pages.

WINNING WAYS FOR WORKING CHURCHES—By Roy L. Smith. The Abingdon Press, 1932. 240 pages.

JOURNALISM IN GENERAL

ART OF PLAIN TALK, THE—By Rudolf Flesch. Harper & Bros., N.Y., 1946. 210 pages. Tells you how to speak and write so that people understand what you mean. A popularization of Dr. Flesch's doctoral dissertation on readability.

FUNDAMENTALS OF JOURNALISM—By Ivan Benson. Prentice-Hall, Inc., N.Y., 1937. 329 pages. A good journalism textbook.

NEWS GATHERING AND NEWS WRITING—By Robert M. Neal. Prentice-Hall, Inc., N.Y., 1940. 566 pages. As fascinating a journalistic textbook as has ever been written and as unlike a textbook as one could imagine. The author teaches by narrative method.

NEWSPAPER EDITING, MAKE-UP AND HEADLINE—By Norman J. Radder and John E. Stempel. McGraw-Hill Book Co., N.Y., 1942. 398 pages. Technical and professional.

OUTLINE SURVEY OF JOURNALISM, AN—By J. F. Mott and others. Barnes & Noble, Inc., N.Y.C., 1940. 381 pages (paper-bound). A valuable course in journalism, closely packed, written by professors from several schools.

PUBLICITY IN GENERAL

HOW TO GET PUBLICITY—By Milton Wright. McGraw-Hill Book Co., Inc., N.Y., 1935. 220 pages. Deals largely with newspapers and periodicals.

PRESS AGENTRY—By Charles Washburn, well-known press agent. National Library Press, N.Y.C., 1937. 153 pages. Experiences related center largely in promotion of theatrical productions and personalities. Includes chapter containing valuable suggestions from editors.

PRINCIPLES OF PUBLICITY—By Quiett and Casey. Appleton & Co., 1926. 400 pages. A modern and comprehensive publicity textbook. Contains a chapter on church publicity.

PUBLICITY—HOW TO PLAN, PRODUCE AND PLACE IT—By Herbert M. Baus. Harper & Bros., N.Y.C., 1942. 245 pages. A book of practical help to those who handle publicity and are interested in its technique, and for those also whose lives or business are influenced by public opinion and who wish to know more about the forces behind it.

SO YOU'RE PUBLICITY CHAIRMAN—By Frances Fiske. Whittlesey House, N.Y.C., 1940. 183 pages. Very practical, also entertaining. Written from the standpoint of women's club member.

PUBLIC RELATIONS

BLUEPRINT FOR PUBLIC RELATIONS—By Dwight Hillis Plackard & Clifton Blackmon. McGraw-Hill Book Co., Inc., N.Y.C., 1947. 355 pages. Expert public relations counsel.

PUBLIC RELATIONS—By Sills and Lesly. Richard D. Irwin, Inc., 1945. 321 pages. A thoroughly practical book containing many valuable suggestions.

YOU AND YOUR PUBLIC—By Verne Burnett, Harper & Bros., N.Y.C., 1943. 194 pages. A highly human and personal discussion of how to deal with the various publics.

RADIO

RELIGIOUS RADIO—What To Do and How—By Everett C. Parker, Elinor Inman and Ross Snyder. Harper & Bros., N.Y.C., 1948. 272 pages. It is doubtful if any three people know more about religious radio than these authors. Programming, motivation, script writing and production.

MISCELLANEOUS

FUNDAMENTALS OF MIMEOGRAPH STENCIL DUPLICATION—edited by Dr. Peter L. Agnew. A. B. Dick Co., Chicago, 1947. A practical manual on stencil preparation, machine operation and the uses of mimeographing.

HOW TO WRITE SIGNS, TICKETS, AND POSTERS—By Hasluck. David McKay Co., Philadelphia. 160 pages. Just what its name implies. (paper-bound)

SUCCESSFUL LETTERS FOR CHURCHES—By Stewart Harral. Abingdon-Cokesbury, 1946. 247 pages.

YOUR CREATIVE POWER, How to Use Imagination—By Alex F. Osborn. Charles Scribner's Sons, N.Y.C., 1948. 375 pages. Gives specific ways to develop your creative and imaginative powers. The various techniques explained and documented will enable you to discover, adapt, and create ways of exposing more people to the influence of Christ and the services of His church. The author of "Building Up Your Congregation" is a product of Mr. Osborn's creative training.

Dear Heavenly Father support us all the day long, till the shadows lengthen and the evening comes, and the busy world is hushed and fever of life is over, and our work is done. Then in Thy mercy give us a safe lodging . . . a holy rest . . . and peace at the last.

Index

*** Sources of information and materials.**

Know Your Congregation as Business Knows Its Customers

PLAN SHEET

Essential Information on Congregations

. Official Number of Contributing Members

Year	*Number of Members*	*Gain or Loss over Preceding Year*
19	....	....
19	....	....
19	....	....
19	....	....
19	....	....

2. New Members of Congregation

Year	*Adults*	*From Sunday School*	*Total Gain*
19	....	....	....
19	....	....	....
19	....	....	....
19	....	....	....
19	....	....	....

3. Members Lost to Congregation

Year	*Deaths*	*Transfers to Other Churches*	*Members Who Stopped Contributing*	*Total of All Losses*
19	....	....	....	....
19	....	....	....	....
19	....	....	....	....
19	....	....	....	....

4. Size of Sunday School

Year	*Registered Members of the Schools*	*Gain or Loss over Previous Year*
19	....	....
19	....	....
19	....	....
19	....	....

5. Attendance at Church Services

Year	*Average Attendance at Sunday Services*	*Gain or Loss*
19	....	....
19	....	....
19	....	....
19	....	....

PLAN SHEET
Building Larger Congregations

Special Service	*Date of Service*	*Chairman in Charge*
unders' Day	....	....
ood Neighbor Sunday	....	....
hurch School Sunday	....	....
edical Sunday	....	....
ower Sunday	....	....
irl Scout Sunday	....	....
oy Scout Sunday	....	....
ampfire Girl Sunday	....	....
ducational Sunday	....	....
o-to-Church Sunday	....	....
aymen's Sunday	....	....
hurch Decoration Night	....	....
emorial Service	....	....
ther Special Sundays	....	....
....	....	....
....	....	....
....	....	....
....	....	....
....	....	....
....	....	....
....	....	....
....	....	....
....	....	....
....	....	....
....	....	....

Keeping the Away-at-School Crowd Going to Church

PLAN SHEET

Keeping the Away-at-School Crowd Going to Church

1. *Getting Addresses of Out-of-Town Students*

   Chairman: ....

2. *Writing Letters to Ministers in School Cities*

   Chairman: ....

3. *Writing to Students Away at School*

   Chairman of Committee: ....

   Dates of Letters ....

4. *Sending Church Bulletins to Students*

   Dates When Bulletins Will be Sent:

   ....

   ....

5. *Holiday Social Functions for Students*

   Chairman: ....

   Date for Christmas Gathering ....

   Date for Easter Gathering ....

   Other Gatherings ....

6. *September Service for Students and Families*

   Chairman: ....

   Date ....

Building Attendance Through Better Singing

PLAN SHEET

Building Attendance Through Better Singing

1. Date of Survey on Favorite Hymns ....
2. Chairman of Survey Committee ....
3. Dates for Congregation Hymn Practice

   ....

   ....

   ....

   ....

4. Dates for Youth Choir at Regular Service

   ....

   ....

5. Date for Annual Choir Sunday ....
6. Possible Contributors of Crosses for Choir

   ....

   ....

7. Other Plans for Improving Congregational Singing

   ....

   ....

   ....

   ....

   ....

   ....

Reselling a Church to Its Members

PLAN SHEET

Increasing Financial Support

1. *Amount Pledged* ....

Amount Paid ....

Year	*Total Amount*	*Gain or Loss over Previous Year*
19	....	....
19	....	....
19	....	....
19	....	....

2. *Average Contribution*

	Average Pledge or Paid	*Comparison with Year Before*
19	....	....
19	....	....
19	....	....
19	....	....

3. *Plans to Increase Pledges*

Loyalty Sunday Program

Date ....

Chairman ....

Committee Members

....

....

....

4. *People to Work on Booklet,* Letters, and Other Announcements

....

....

....

....

....

....

....

5. *Ideas for Thank-you Letter*

....

....

....

....

....

6. *Other Ideas for Building Church Support*

....

....

....

....

....

....

7. *Material for Which to Send*

....

....

....

Use a Basic Theme

PLAN SHEET

Publicizing the Basic Theme

"Churchgoing Families are Happier Families"
(or other basic theme)

People to notify and things to do in order that the above theme be included in the following:

1. On Outside Church Bulletin Board

....
....
....

2. On Printed Weekly Church Bulletin

....
....
....
....
....

3. On Inside Church Bulletin Board

....
....
....

4. On Individual Boxes for Pledge Envelopes

....
....
....

5. At Bottom of Church Letterheads

....
....
....

6. On Outside Church Identification Name Plate

....
....
....

7. Painted on Wall of Main Sunday School Room

....
....
....
....
....

8. Added to Base of Church Advertisements When Space Permits

....
....
....

9. Included in Sermons Whenever Logical and Possible

....
....
....

PLAN SHEET

Publicizing Your Church

1. *Publicity Committee*
   Chairman: ....
   Committee Members: ....
   ....
   ....
   ....

2. *Activities or Events to Be Publicized*
   ....
   ....

3. *Bulletin Board Committee*
   ....
   ....

4. *Contact with "Home-Church-School" Foundation*
   ....

5. *Committee for Roadside Bulletin*
   ....
   ....

6. *Chairman in Charge of Newspaper Announcements*
   ....

7. *Other Promotional Activities*
   ....
   ....

Start Your Plans Today

PLAN SHEET

Other Promotional Plans That Work

1. Installation, and/or Greater Use of Outside Bulletin Board
   ....
   ....
   ....

2. & 3. Invitation Sign in Hotel Lobbies and Pickup for Guests
   ....
   ....
   ....

4. & 5. Guest Book for Vestibule and Free Post Cards
   Chairman ....
   ....
   ....

6. Outside-of-City Bulletin for Visitors, Tourists
   ....
   ....
   ....

8. (Outside) Flying of Church Flag
   ....
   ....
   ....

9. Additional Ringing of Church Bell
   ....
   ....
   ....

10. Illumination of Spire and of Windows
    Chairman ....
    ....
    ....

11. Arrangements for a Church Garden
    Chairman ....
    ....
    ....

Additional Ideas and Suggestions

2. Books of Sermons
   ....
   ....
   ....

3. Subjects for Sermon Series
   ....
   ....
   ....

4. Literature Rack
   Chairman ....
   ....
   ....

9. Calling on Prisons
   Chairman ....
   ....
   ....

10. District Plan for Visiting
    Chairman ....
    ....
    ....

11. Use-of-Literature Portfolio
    ....
    ....
    ....

Note: Numbers refer to numbered sections in Chapters 20 and 21.